Druids on The Silk Road:
Independent Wales in a Changing World

Emlyn Phillips MSc MBA PGCert

First published 2024
by Rowanvale Books Ltd
The Gate
Keppoch Street
Roath
Cardiff
CF24 3JW
www.rowanvalebooks.com

A CIP catalogue record for this book is available from the British Library.
ISBN: 978-1-83584-045-0

To the memory of my late parents, June and Graham Phillips of Cowbridge, for their constant love and support.

CONTENTS

FOREWORD

Two of the essays in this collection – 'Wales and the Silk Road' and 'Welsh and the End of the Modern World' – were first published in the much-missed magazine *Planet: The Welsh Internationalist*, the former winning their 2022 New Writer competition. 'The Fall of Môn' was first published on a now-defunct blog. 'Rebuilding a Welsh Civilisation' and 'Druids on the Silk Road' are new for this collection. The rest were first published by the online magazine *Bylines Cymru*. However, the versions in this collection may differ in some respects from the versions that were published. I would like to thank Emily Trahair, the former editor of *Planet*, and Dr Rachel Morris, the editor of *Bylines Cymru*, for their encouragement and support.

REBUILDING A WELSH CIVILISATION

The year 1826 saw the death of the stonemason, antiquarian, poet, anti-slavery activist and Unitarian organiser Edward Williams, better known as Iolo Morganwg.

Iolo's lifetime had seen the Welsh language surge back into his beloved Glamorgan. After a period in which English had been gaining ground – particularly in the southern Vale – the county, whose population had only recently overtaken that of Carmarthenshire, was almost completely Welsh-speaking.

A century later, in 1926, the situation had changed. The industrialisation of South Wales had initially drawn its workforce from elsewhere in Wales itself, building strong, Welsh-speaking working-class communities. Over time, though, the influx increasingly came from England, and Glamorgan – which was by now far and away the most populous area of Wales – had become overwhelmingly Anglophone.

In Iolo's day, the United Kingdom was almost completely self-sufficient, producing nearly everything it needed. England had lost most of its colonies in North America but had hung on to Canada and some islands in the Caribbean. Its control over Australia was being consolidated but it had not yet claimed New Zealand. In Africa, it had a toehold in the Cape Colony, centred on Cape Town, but little else. In India, British control was expanding, but this was being done by the privately owned East India Company, not the British state – which was still organised much as it had been in Tudor times, with no civil service to speak of and most administration carried out at the local level.

Wales and England maintained their separate identities, with the Welsh language still commonly referred to as 'the British tongue', acknowledging its cultural continuity from the ancient world – but anti-Welsh sentiment was a powerful force amongst the English. Iolo and his peers were already worried about the future. They were aware that the remaining Welsh gentry families were dying out and their estates being bought by Englishmen who had no sympathy for Welsh culture. Their libraries, which had preserved ancient manuscripts, were being lost or destroyed; the poetic tradition of the bards was being forgotten. Iolo responded as best he could: partly by collecting documents, but most effectively by developing a new national myth. Drawing inspiration from history, he revived Owain Glyndŵr's vision of Welsh national institutions; he himself reinvigorated the National Eisteddfod by establishing the Gorsedd of Bards, creating a vehicle for intellectual and cultural vitality.

By 1926, things looked very different. London had created a professional civil service in 1870, and government had become much more centralised. England now ruled vast areas of the world and did so through the apparatus of empire. Ownership of a 'British' identity had been wrested from the Welsh and was now applied to an imperial, English-dominated, state. Many of the Welsh bought into this, particularly the increasing numbers who could not speak the language: this new 'Britishness' provided a sense of identity for those who were neither English nor Cymry Cymraeg. London had immediately put its new organisation to work to shape this empire in its own image. Most importantly, all of the Crown's subjects should speak English. This was particularly the case in Wales; the traditional English antipathy towards a separate Welsh identity and language had been deepened by revolts against the British establishment in the form of the Scotch Cattle, the Rebecca Rioters, the Merthyr Uprising and the Chartists. This rebellion had to be stopped and the power of the state was deployed to ensure it did – most effectively, through the education system.

Equally corrosive were economic developments. British manufacturing and industry were still vastly important but the resources it used now came from the Empire, as did most of the workforce's dietary staples, such as wheat. Coal mining in Wales was in decline – it was increasingly uneconomical – but it was still the bedrock of the communities and culture of South Wales.

These economic pressures, combined with the English-focused education, were changing the Welsh sense of self. More and more, as socialism took root, the miners and workers in the other 'smokestack industries' defined themselves in terms of class and internationalism, not nationality and traditional identity. The change was widely noted at the time. In 1926, Saunders Lewis delivered a lecture to the newly formed National Party of Wales, arguing that the priority for the Welsh nationalist movement should not be independence but rather the revival – or re-creation – of a distinctively Welsh civilisation.[1] This was not to be based on race, nor depend on the structures of a state – be that an independent Wales or a Wales still chained within the British Empire. It was to be based on the Welsh language and its unbroken continuity with the past.[2] In this, Saunders Lewis's vision was much the same as that of Iolo Morganwg.

One of Lewis's key points was that South Wales should be de-industrialised. Agriculture and rural industries should become the basis of the Welsh economy.[3] This was a radical notion indeed – so radical as to seem completely unrealistic. The mining industry may have been in decline, with its communities already suffering mass unemployment and the emigration of thousands of their inhabitants to England or elsewhere in the empire, but even so, coal and other heavy industries were core to the identity and self-image of Wales in the inter-war period. In 1921, shortly before Lewis spoke, the population of the Rhondda Valley alone was 167,000; four decades earlier, it had been only 55,000. Overall, Wales in 1921 had a total of 271,000 miners.[4] Add to that their family members, and it is obvious that Lewis and his party were calling for the impossible. The mining communities of South Wales were already in trouble, but the industry was still working, the communities were still vibrant, and there was a powerful sense of a South Walian Anglo-Welsh identity that would later be expressed by the likes of Dylan Thomas and the rest of the 'Kardomah Gang'. How could all of that be swept away?

Indeed, in 1929, the poet Robert Graves – who had served in the trenches with the Royal Welch Fusiliers and was a noted writer on Celtic myth – commented that the Welsh had been transformed from an untameable, essentially pre-modern people as passionately committed to personal freedom as to they were to their language, their culture and their hills, into an industrial, chapel-going working class who had abandoned their old myths in favour of a new culture hero: the English-speaking miner. [5] Of Lewis and Graves, Graves was undoubtedly the more accurate in his observations – at the time.

Derrick Hearne, writing in the 1970s, believed that Saunders Lewis's focus on culture and a 'Welsh civilisation' was completely wrong: a focus on political independence above all was needed. Hearne contrasted Lewis's thinking with the 'activist' approach, which Hearne identified with the methods of Lewis's contemporary, D. J. Davies. Davies, Hearne argued, was goal-oriented, practical and firmly rooted in the industrial society of mid-twentieth century Wales. [6] Lewis himself went to his grave believing that he had failed utterly. [7]

So how about today, a century after Lewis delivered his lecture? The British Empire is long gone, British industry and manufacturing are mostly gone, and the residual frameworks that continued to pump the world's resources into the living standards of the British population are collapsing. Lewis's vision of a de-industrialised South Wales has become a reality, not through the policies of Welsh nationalism but through the contemptuous indifference of Westminster. The Rhondda has no working pits and no colliers; the de-industrialised mining communities now stand out as the most deprived areas of Wales and amongst the poorest in the UK.[8] The working class is no longer working, clinging to the only place it knows through a combination of the dole, long-term disability payments and government-funded antidepressants.[9]

Indeed, Anglo-Welsh culture has already collapsed to the point where youths deliberately set fire to schools so that they can entertain themselves by pelting the firemen with stones,[10] and the use of illegal drugs has become normalised.[11] In the Valleys, and even in the capital city, the Anglo-Welsh social fabric has decayed to the extent that those who have nothing can only seek fulfilment through nihilistic destruction of the society around them.[12] The industries have gone, but the people and the communities remain, and despite decades of effort, no one has found a new economic foundation to replace the old one. The collier and his culture, which inspired both Robert Graves and D. J. Davies in their different ways, have vanished, while Davies's 'activist' approach – so admired by Derrick Hearne – has brought Welsh independence and a prosperous Welsh society little closer to reality than they were in the days of David Lloyd

George and Cymru Fydd. It seems that the passage of time has vindicated Saunders Lewis.

What's more, the Welsh language is returning. It offers a sense of self, a source of pride – and economic opportunity.[13] Across the border, English identity is undergoing a revival, in both positive and negative ways. Here, a generally positive sense of Welsh identity is also reviving, particularly aware of our language and heritage; the decision to use the Welsh names for some of our national parks is an indication of this. It is also, however, an indication of the decline of the imperial British identity. The English-speaking Welsh (are they still referred to as 'Anglo-Welsh'? I'll use the term) are being squeezed; the overarching imperial state they identified with is gone, as are the economic foundations of the culture that maintained a distinct Anglo-Welsh identity. It seems increasingly inevitable that this identity will decline.

It is also true that the Valleys are one of the regions that most strongly identify as Welsh.[14] This maintenance of two separate senses of identity was possible while both Britain and Wales could be regarded as separate and distinct things;[15] holding dual nationality isn't exactly uncommon, after all. As 'Britishness' evaporates, though, with the economic foundations of the old industrial communities gone or going, and 'Welshness' becomes once again strongly associated with the Welsh language, what identity remains for the declining communities of Anglo-Wales, who increasingly derive their cultural references from the London media and the global internet?

In this collection of essays, I'm afraid that I make no attempt to answer this question; it's a problem that needs to be addressed by people more familiar with these communities than I am, and who are more qualified to speak on their behalf.

My intention is to pick up Lewis's challenge. Like him, like Iolo, I believe that we need to re-establish a distinctly Welsh civilisation. Not one that continues with the old 'British' worldview expressed in Welsh, but something different; a worldview that, as in Lewis's vision, reflects and continues that which existed when Wales was a distinct polity within a patchwork of other polities – polities within Europe, and polities far beyond, running along the Silk Road to the far reaches of Asia. Establishing this civilisational outlook will mean building pride in our language and culture, of course, but it also means decolonising the way we think: not only in terms of the fading 'cultural cringe' towards Anglo-American culture, but also in shedding the sense of superiority and privilege relative to the rest of the world which was a feature of imperial Britishness.

This isn't in the least sense a romantic project. Let me emphasise that. It's an absolutely essential response to the rapid and dramatic changes in the world we live in. It's a first step towards dealing with the consequences of climate change, the consequences of global resource depletion and the consequences of the ongoing shift in political and economic power away from the declining states of the West and towards the re-emerging cultures of Eurasia, Africa and the Americas.

To do this, we need to change the stories we tell ourselves about who we are and how we live in the world. The myth of the miner identified by Robert Graves had its moment and then slipped away. It's time for us to turn back to our older myths and heroes, which have endured and inspired us for millennia. It's time to review our history for what it can teach us about ourselves as a distinct people and civilisation – one of the patches in the cultural patchwork not just of Europe but of the wider world. It's time to unify the civilisational thinking of Saunders Lewis with the goal-orientation of D. J. Davies in order to steer Wales through the transition to a multi-polar, resource-depleted world of global weirding.

In this collection of essays, I hope to contribute to different ways of thinking about Welshness and the way we will live. I hope to contribute to the policy discussions about deepening and broadening the use of the Welsh language.

Let's talk about Welsh dragons on the Silk Road…

ENDNOTES

[1] Lewis, S. (1926). 'Egwyddorion Cenedlaetholdeb.' Lecture delivered at the Plaid Cymru summer school. Published 1975 as 'Egwyddorion Cenedlaetholdeb - Principles of Nationalism.' Translated by Bruce Griffiths. Cardiff: Plaid Cymru.

[2] Jones, R. M. (2003). 'Wales and British Politics, 1900–1939' in Wrigley, C. (ed.) *A Companion to Early Twentieth-Century Britain*. Oxford: Blackwell. pp.87–101. pp.96–97.

[3] Plaid Cymru (1937). Cymru Rydd: Braslun o Bolisi'r Blaid Genedlaethol. Caernarfon: Sywddfa'r Blaid Genedlaethol. pp.12–13.

[4] Jones, R. M. (2003). 'Wales and British Politics, 1900–1939' in Wrigley, C. (ed.) *A Companion to Early Twentieth-Century Britain*. Oxford: Blackwell. pp.87–101. p.89.

[5] Graves, R. (1929). *Goodbye to All That*, p.75 cited in Jones, R. M. (1992) 'Beyond Identity? The Reconstruction of the Welsh'. *Journal of British Studies*, 31 (4) pp.330–357, p.331. Graves removed this passage from the heavily revised second edition of his book, which was published in 1958.

6   Hearne, D. K. (1977). *The Joy of Freedom*. Talybont: Y Lolfa. pp.59–64.

7   Jones, D. (1996). '"I Failed Utterly": Saunders Lewis and the Cultural Politics of Welsh Modernism.' *The Irish Review* (Cork) 19: 22–43.

8   Office for National Statistics (2022). Household deprivation – Census Maps, *ONS*. www.ons.gov.uk. https://www.ons.gov.uk/census/maps/choropleth/population/household-deprivation/hh-deprivation/household-is-not-deprived-in-any-dimension?oa=W00008735

9   Easton, M. (2013). 'The unbearable sadness of the Welsh valleys'. *BBC News*. 25 Jun. https://www.bbc.co.uk/news/magazine-23028078

10   (i) BBC News (2015). '30 youths throw stones at fire crew in Cwmbran'. *BBC News*. 2 Aug. https://www.bbc.co.uk/news/uk-wales-south-east-wales-33751851

     (ii) BBC News (2019). 'Stones thrown at police and fire crews in Phillipstown'. *BBC News*. 12 Jan. https://www.bbc.co.uk/news/uk-wales-46851815

     (iii) BBC News (2022). 'Caerphilly: Firefighters attacked by youths throwing stones'. *BBC News*. Apr. https://www.bbc.co.uk/news/uk-wales-60959064

11   (i) The Guardian (2001). 'Heroin epidemic grips the valleys'. *The Guardian*. 1 Apr. https://www.theguardian.com/society/2001/apr/01/drugsandalcohol

     (ii) BBC News (2002). 'Valleys struggle against drugs "epidemic"'. newsimg.bbc.co.uk. https://newsimg.bbc.co.uk/1/hi/wales/2360559.stm

(iii) Parveen, N. (2019). 'Llanelli hit by wave of "county lines" drug gangs'. *The Guardian*. https://www.theguardian.com/uk-news/2019/feb/15/llanelli-hit-by-wave-of-county-lines-drug-gangs

(iv) Ren (2021). 'Drug Addiction and Overdose Statistics Surge in Wales'. *Narconon United Kingdom*. https://www.narcononuk.org.uk/blog/drug-addiction-and-overdose-statistics-surge-in-wales.html

12 (i) Grey, J. and Local Democracy Reporting Service (2023). 'Nextbike Cardiff: Bike sharing scheme scrapped due to theft'. *BBC News*. 8 Dec. https://www.bbc.co.uk/news/uk-wales-67646004

(ii) Price, E. (2023). 'One of the new stations in Merthyr Tydfil which is…'. *X* (formerly *Twitter*). https://x.com/EPriceJourno/status/1730865587801260397

13 Janes, E. (2023). Welsh language in the Valleys: is it really down in the pits? *Life360*. https://cardiffjournalism.co.uk/life360/welsh-language-in-the-valleys-is-it-really-down-in-the-pits/

14 Welsh Government (2023). National identity by area and identity. statswales.gov.wales. https://statswales.gov.wales/Catalogue/Equality-and-Diversity/National-Identity/nationalidentity-by-area-identity

15 Wyn Jones, R. (2014). *The Fascist Party in Wales? Plaid Cymru, Welsh Nationalism, and the Accusation of Fascism*. Cardiff: University of Wales Press. pp.69–70.

WALES AND THE SILK ROAD

What connects the ancient Druids and the Buddha, Alexander the Great, Edward Longshanks and Kubilai Khan, the Pharaohs and today's cost-of-living crisis? What does this connection have to do with Iolo Morganwg? And what does it mean for Wales today?

Let's begin by picturing Afghanistan. Not the impoverished, wounded country we see on the news today, though. Picture instead the Afghanistan of two millennia ago: a larger country, then known as Bactria, which extended into modern-day Tajikistan, Uzbekistan and the Punjab region. Bactria was rich – a wealth derived from fertile lands and oases and, even more so, its position on the Silk Road. Bactria was a central-Asian hub on the trade routes that have transported goods and ideas between the distant edges of Eurasia since time immemorial. Its famously beautiful capital city, Balkh, was just one of a string of glorious cities including Xi'an, Kashgar, Tashkent and Samarkand, Baghdad, Smyrna, Constantinople and Rome.

Bactria's wealth attracted Alexander the Great, who conquered it in 256 BC. He created a new kingdom where Greek and Indian cultures merged to create something new: a country of Greek-speaking Buddhists.[1] Coins of these Greco-Buddhist kings, including some issued by King Menander, have been found in Britain – a number in Wales, or near Stonehenge.[2] Menander reigned a century before Julius Caesar visited Britain: two centuries before the Emperor Claudius invaded. People were thus travelling between a still-Druidic Celtic Britain and Greco-Buddhist Bactria.

That may seem unlikely to us, but it shouldn't. Cultural influences between the western and eastern ends of Eurasia can be traced back for many millennia: Ötzi the Iceman, whose body was discovered in the Alps, has tattoos at points used in Chinese acupuncture.[3] The mummified bodies of Tocharian people buried many centuries ago in Xinjiang, where China blurs into Central Asia, show that they were red-haired with blue eyes, and wore fabrics very similar to examples preserved from the Celtic Hallstatt period.[4] In the days of the Druids, Greek colonies existed all around the Mediterranean, the Black Sea, and onwards to Afghanistan. Along the way, in what is now Türkiye, was a powerful Celtic kingdom – Galatia. Galatian warriors were famous mercenaries; they served, amongst many others, the Pharaohs of ancient Egypt – including the Ptolemies, descended from Greeks.

We know from Classical authors that some Druids spoke Greek. For them, a journey from Britain to Bactria would have been a series of hops from one Greek colony to another, with a stay amongst their fellow Celts in Galatia at the halfway point. Starting in Marseille and ending in Balkh would have been a long and arduous journey, of

course, but they would have known where they were
going and would have had local guides for each stage
who had made the journey many times.

These travel routes remained open for many centuries.
In the second century AD, Clemens – a Christian from
Greek-speaking Alexandria in Roman Egypt – wrote that
his teacher, Pantaenus, had visited India, studying there
before returning to Egypt.[5] In the sixth century, Christian
monks who had been living in India and learned about silk
production there, went to China on behalf of the Emperor
Justinian; they returned to Constantinople with stolen
silkworm eggs, thus enabling Europeans to produce silk
for the first time.[6]

In 1288, Edward I of England met the emissary of a
Mongol Khan to discuss a military alliance against the
Muslim Mameluke empire of Egypt.[7] The emissary was
Rabban Bar Sauma, a Christian bishop.[8] Rabban had
been sent by Arghun, the Mongol ruler of Persia (who
himself was a Buddhist), but he had been born in China:
Rabban was a Uighur, and a subject of Kubilai Khan –
the same Kubilai who was playing host to a Venetian,
Marco Polo, at the same time. The Anglo-Mongol alliance
did not happen: Edward decided to attack the Welsh and
Scots, not the Mamelukes. What would Wales be like if
he had chosen differently? Rabban eventually died in
Baghdad, having repeatedly travelled through Central
Asia, the Middle East and Europe. No one thought him
unusual, because he wasn't.

This traffic across Eurasia only ended after 1453, when
the Ottoman Turks stormed Constantinople, stopping

the flow of goods along the Silk Road and depriving Europeans of the spices and luxuries to which they had been accustomed for so many thousands of years.

The world changed. Within a generation, Columbus – seeking a new source of spices – had landed in the Americas. The Welshman Henry VII and his descendants would bring Britain out of the Middle Ages and begin its transformation into a modern state. Europe began its rise to global dominance: a dominance based on sea power and oceanic travel. The cities of the Silk Road fell into obscurity and poverty, sad shadows of their past glory. Europeans forgot that that their ancestors had once travelled those roads.

Europe's empires grew quickly as they sought the world's resources. Spain and Portugal were first, stripping the wealth of South America and making the first inroads into India and south-east Asia. Within a century and a half, they were exhausted and were supplanted by the rising powers of northern Europe – England, France and the Netherlands.

And this brings us to Iolo Morganwg. Born in 1747, he saw the modern world being forged by revolution upon revolution. The Agricultural Revolution fuelled population growth, while the Industrial Revolution was beginning to transform technology. The American Revolution produced the United States, while the French Revolution led to Napoleon, whose armies introduced a common, scientific system of measurement and a system of civil law across Europe. In Iolo's lifetime, many indigenous cultures of North America remained untouched by European power. In India, the Mughal Empire and many Hindu states were still being treated as equals by the East India Company. In Africa, the slave trade had caused devastation, but there had been little attempt by Europeans to take control of territory.

Iolo died long before the British Empire reached its full extent, but the trends were clear. In Wales, as in its colonies in Asia and Africa, London intended to stamp out local languages and culture so as to make the world English. Iolo understood that peoples and cultures need myths to live by, stories to explain who they are and what to value. His enduring triumph is that he gave the Welsh new myths: myths that were powerful enough to sustain them and enable them to endure the 'imperial century' when London's rule spanned the globe.[9]

The Silk Road teaches us to take a long view of history. Empires rise, then fall. In Menander's Bactria, Timur's Samarkand, Ptolemy's Egypt and Justinian's Constantinople, most people surely imagined that their society would last forever. Few people really believe that their way of life will one day vanish – but it always does, and it's rarely pleasant for those who go through it. Sometimes, everything changes forever in a day – like May 29th, 1453, when Ottoman armies broke the gates of Constantinople. Sometimes, it takes generations, such as the slow decline of many kingdoms along the Silk Road. Every year, things get a bit worse and a bit different, until, without really noticing it, the people and their society have become something new, no longer who they used to be.

We Welsh are in the second group. We survived the end of Rome and the Saxon invasions. We survived the

Normans and the British Empire at its height. We have adapted to changing circumstances, but we are still the people of Caratacus and of Cunedda – and of Magnus Maximus. Now, the world is changing again, and so must we.

The British Empire formally ended decades ago, but its economic systems, designed to extract cheap resources from Asia and Africa, have continued to work just as they were intended – until now. Largely unreported by the British media, a great realignment in the global economy is taking place. The ancient civilisation-states of Eurasia – China, Russia, Iran and India – are integrating their economies more and more closely, for the benefit of their own societies. They are being joined by the resource-rich states of Central Asia, the energy states of the Persian Gulf, more and more African states and others in South America. Türkiye and Balkan states, and others from southern and eastern Europe are joining as they lose faith in the EU project. The mechanisms by which this is happening overlap – the Eurasian Economic Union, the Shanghai Cooperation Organisation, the BRICS and the Belt and Road Initiative – but we can group them under one label: the reborn Silk Road.

All of these countries are tired of being exploited for the benefit of Western economies and are now doing something about it.[10] [11] [12] [13] The result will be a return to the historical state of affairs: wealth lies in the East. In the days of Rome, the emperors fretted about the amounts of silver being spent to buy Asian imports.[14] The Spanish kings worried about the wealth leaving Mexico for the

Philippines and China, rather than for Spain.[15] Europe may well become what it always was: a relatively poor and unimportant peninsula of no great concern to most of Eurasia. For a historically brief period, we had the military and economic strength to shape the world for our benefit; we don't any longer, and we'll just have to get used to that.

And there lies the problem. Wales is still ruled by an inward-looking London elite that is increasingly out of touch with this reality – and acknowledging reality is critical. One of Iolo's enduring slogans was 'The Truth against the world', and it's very relevant today. The new world coming into view may very well not be what we want. It may mean dealing with governments we do not like, and whose values conflict with our own. It will definitely mean that we, individually and as a Welsh nation, will be poorer and our standard of living will be lower. Our cost-of-living crisis is only beginning, because the societies that have resources and industries will increasingly keep their wealth for themselves. This is the objective reality that we will have to deal with, because we cannot prevent it. We must acknowledge the truth of what is happening in the world.

Iolo Morganwg lived at a time when European imperialism was in its early stages. Today, we live in a time when that imperialism is in its death throes. As Iolo understood, when dealing with a new reality, we need new myths – or new interpretations of the old ones. More than two thousand years ago, our Celtic ancestors dealt on equal terms with the cultures of the Far East. What narratives will show us as the heirs of those Druids who journeyed to central Asia? What bonds will we establish to connect Bangor with Bukhara, Aberystwyth with Almaty, Swansea with Samarkand, and Cardiff with Cochin? What stories will show us the way forward in a world dominated by the East rather than the West? We need to be creative now. If we can rise to the challenge, the future of Wales may be very interesting indeed.

ENDNOTES

1 Thapar, R. & Kurth, A. (2012). 'Indo Grccks'. In *The Oxford Classical Dictionary*. Oxford University Press. https://www.oxfordreference.com/view/10.1093/acref/9780199545568.001.0001/acref-9780199545568-e-3280

2 Green, C. (2016). 'Indo-Greek, Indo-Scythian & other early Indian coins found in Britain'. https://www.caitlingreen.org/2015/01/indo-greek-indo-scythian-other-early.html

3 Pabst, M. A., Letofsky-Pabst, I., Bock, E., Moser, M., Dorfer, L., Egarter-Vigl, E. & Hofer, F. (2009). 'The tattoos of the Tyrolean Iceman: a light microscopical, ultrastructural and element analytical study' in *Journal of Archaeological Science*, 36 (4).

4 Barber, E. W. (1999). *The Mummies of Ürümchi*. MacMillan.

5 St. Jerome (1999). *On Illustrious Men (The Fathers of the Church series, Vol. 100)*. Translated by Halton, T. P. (1999). The Catholic University of America Press.

6   Procopius (2010). *The Secret History: with Related Texts*. Edited & translated by Kaldellis, A. Hackett Publishing Company, Inc.

7   Encyclopædia Britannica. (n.d.). 'Arghūn'. *Britannica Academic*. https://academic.eb.com/levels/collegiate/article/Argh%C5%ABn/9378

8   Encyclopædia Britannica. (n.d.). 'Rabban bar Sauma'. *Britannica Academic*. https://academic.eb.com/levels/collegiate/article/Rabban-bar-Sauma/13252

9   Hyam, R. & Low, D. A. (2002). *Britain's Imperial Century, 1815–1914: A Study of Empire and Expansion*. 3rd edition. Palgrave Macmillan Limited.

10   Devonshire-Ellis, C. (2021). 'Egypt & Saudi Arabia to Join Shanghai Cooperation Organisation As Dialogue Partners'. *Silk Road Briefing*. https://www.silkroadbriefing.com/news/2021/09/01/egypt-saudi-arabia-to-join-shanghai-cooperation-organisation-as-dialogue-partners/

11   Das, D. (2022). 'Jaishankar Calls Out "Europe's Problem Is World's Problem" Mindset; Holds India's Ground'. 3 Jun. republicworld.com https://www.republicworld.com/world-news/global-event-news/jaishankar-calls-out-europes-problem-is-worlds-problem-mindset-holds-indias-ground-articleshow.html

12   Mutsila, L. (2022). 'South African Will Not Be Bullied: Naledi Pandor Makes SAns Swoon With Her Bold

Stance on Russia-Ukraine War'. 10 Aug. https://briefly. co.za/politics/134906-south-african-bullied-naledi-pandor-sans-swoon-bold-stance-russia-ukrani-war/

13 Anon. (2002). 'BRICS expects Egypt, Saudi Arabia and Turkey to join group soon'. *Middle East Monitor.* 14 July. https://www.middleeastmonitor.com/20220714-brics-expects-egypt-saudi-arabia-and-turkey-to-join-group-soon/

14 Young. G. K. (2001). *Rome's Eastern Trade: International Commerce and Imperial Policy, 31 BC – AD 305.* Routledge.

15 Gordon, P. (2017). *The Silver Way: China, Spanish America and the Birth of Globalisation, 1565–1815.* Penguin.

WELSH AND THE END
OF THE MODERN WORLD

When I began to learn Welsh in my twenties, I encountered remarks that many readers will have heard: that Welsh is a dying language, and that it is unfit for the modern world. The latest census results have caused concern about the future of the language.[1] More, they suggest that the second criticism might be true: Welsh and its associated culture are not suited to the modern world. If they were, they wouldn't be in decline. The first criticism, however, is off the mark. In fact, it is the modern world that is dying; the Welsh language has survived it and may be better placed than people suspect for the future that is emerging.

By 'the modern world' I mean the world of modernity:[2] technologically developed, economically globalised, urban and organisationally complex. It's the world that began when eighteenth-century rationalism met fossil fuels, matured in the age of European empires and, after the age of formal empire, continued to thrive via the neo-imperial economic structures that endured. Above all, it's a world that depends on cheap energy and cheap resources.

People learn and use languages for different reasons, either affective/intrinsic (because they love the language and its culture) or instrumental/extrinsic[3] (for practical benefits). As Robert Fitzhamon conquered Glamorgan in 1075, one of his knights – Payn de Turberville – set his sights on the manor of Coity, near Bridgend. With Turberville and his men-at-arms approaching, Morgan ap Meurig, whose lands they were, seeing how the wind was blowing, emerged from his stronghold and offered a choice: Turberville could win Coity through single combat – or by wedding Morgan's daughter. Turberville chose marriage.[4] It was, no doubt, a practical decision. And yet, the Turbervilles of Coity were, for centuries afterwards, Welsh in language and culture,[5] unlike the descendants of Fitzhamon's other Norman knights. Clearly, Turberville liked what he found.

Eight centuries later, my grandmother's ancestors came to Glamorgan from Somerset, looking for work. They learned Welsh because they had to; few people in the Vale of Glamorgan spoke English, and Welsh was the language of respectability.[6] My grandparents, both born in 1900, farmed a smallholding near Ystradowen, supplying the family shop in the Rhondda. They both spoke Welsh – but they didn't pass the language on to their children. For them, the influence of the Welsh Not was strong, and the language of prestige and advancement was English. Again, it was a functional decision. In the generations between Payn de Turberville and the present day, the dominant language of the Vale has switched between Welsh and English several times, depending on which offered the best prospects.[7] If the use of Welsh today has declined, there is no reason why the change cannot be reversed again. To achieve this, though, Welsh has to either inspire people or offer the best prospects in life – and ideally both.

To grow, it must be demonstrated that the Welsh language and its culture are the best fit for the environment, which is something worth considering briefly. Language is the way in which people describe their environment; in older forms of Welsh, for example, 'glas' encompassed both blue and green. That's rare in European languages but common in the tropics;[8] its appearance in Welsh reflects the intensity of the light in our maritime environment.[9] Culture is our mental representation of the world and how to behave in it. Our myths, our heroes and all the stories we inherit from the past are templates of behaviours, idealised patterns of values and strategies that can be interpreted for the challenges of the present environment.[10] 'Environment' here means more than the natural world, of course; it includes politics, the economy, social trends, technological developments and the law.[11] This has been the problem for Welsh. As 'modernity' advanced, the political decisions that affected Wales were made in English, the laws governing Wales were in English, and employment was largely in English. In the mass-employer heavy industries, and in mining, many could work in Welsh, of course – but to be a manager required English.[12] Technology, particularly IT, is dominated by English. Social activities and the media are have become dominated by global forces – in English.

The effect has been cumulative. As Welsh is used in fewer domains in life, it weakens in those that remain; the language loses prestige, and its speakers lose confidence.[13] Fewer young people want to speak Welsh, even as more of them are taught it.[14] Here in Carmarthenshire, I meet people proud that their ancestors spoke Welsh – but they tell me in English. I go to businesses staffed entirely by native speakers of Welsh who use the language with me when I insist, but speak English to each other. I meet people who tell me that my Welsh is 'too correct', and they're embarrassed to speak their 'Chav-raeg' with me. This is what the loss of linguistic prestige looks like. A few dogged idealists learning the language for affective reasons won't turn the tide; the language has to provide the main avenue to prosperity and status.

And that might happen – because, as I said, 'the modern world' is dying around us. The empty shelves we have seen this year are a sign of it, as are the rising energy costs. Modernity created a global economy, and the global environment is now changing in ways that will transform our way of life. Energy is one example: there is still a lot of oil and natural gas left, but we've used almost everything that is cheap and easy to extract; depletion means fuel and energy will become much more expensive, until economies collapse.[15] Oil-producing countries will act together in their own economic interests, not that of Western economies. The main producers of natural gas seek to create an OPEC equivalent, so gas prices will remain high.[16] The much-touted 'green tech' revolution depends on minerals such as lithium which are found in the Global South. Growing 'resource nationalism' means that these countries intend to keep the refining of these minerals, the manufacturing of the products using them, and as much as possible of the added value for themselves.[17] So, say goodbye to mass-employment manufacturing, heavy industry and a future for the working class. Indeed, Europe's remaining manufacturing is already collapsing as major companies shut down or head elsewhere. As for the middle class, many of their jobs in (for example) the law or accounting are already being replaced by software, and many more will be replaced by AI[18] (which, by the way, can already produce fiction in Welsh[19]). As Western governments become more openly anti-China, we can expect the supply of Chinese students to dry up – so say goodbye as well to Welsh universities and all of the jobs they support. And to all this, we can add the challenges of rising sea levels, increasingly unpredictable weather and the other consequences of climate weirding.

That's all pretty depressing – and anyone clinging on to the hope of maintaining the way of life we've enjoyed since the Second World War should be depressed because, like it or not, it's over. What will emerge over the years to come is a world where other regions – Asia and Africa in particular – will be more prosperous and prestigious than us. It will be a much more local world, much more dependent on local community and production. Goods will be more expensive; food more local and seasonal (and expensive).

In this environment, I am actually hopeful for the future of the Welsh language. Globally, English will be far less of a lingua franca; languages including Chinese, Russian, Hindi, Arabic and Spanish will be used far more, while the varieties of English used in Africa and Asia will diverge more from British English.[20] Translation will become the norm, English will become less necessary, and the conceit that 'everyone speaks English' will no longer be available as a stick with which to beat Welsh.

I mentioned above the role of myth – and it is our myths that will guide the Welsh-speaking community through the turbulent times ahead. We will lose lands to the sea, but our myths remind us that it's happened before.[21] The Celtic languages emerged here in the far west of Europe during the Neolithic Age[22] – and the tales of Caer Ys, Lyonesse and Cantre'r Gwaelod are memories of lands lost after the glaciers melted. Only a very few cultures globally share this length of cultural continuity; the stories passed down will provide reassurance that life can go on, and help with the grief over what has been lost.[23]

Even today, Welsh farmers are in crisis as fuel, fertiliser and animal feed become too expensive.[24] All of these things depend on fossil fuels, and we can expect them to become far more costly. Solar panels and wind turbines can't fertilise the soil – and that's a huge problem because soil fertility in Britain has been dangerously depleted by 'modern' agriculture.[25] The obvious solution is a change to regenerative agriculture[26] with some rewilding – more labour intensive and more communal, providing many more jobs.[27] Far from being a threat to the Welsh language, they could be its saviour. These methods could see the rapid[28] revival of the temperate rainforests which covered Wales until the nineteenth century, when a squirrel could travel the length of the Rhondda Valley without leaving the branches; the forests that were the setting for the tales of the Mabinogion – tales set in named places, which connect Welsh language and culture firmly to places still inhabited.[29] This could revitalise rural communities – and do so in Welsh.

The schools have their role in this. With the industries of the future unclear and fewer universities (and less need for them), let's imagine Welsh-language schools adopting the proven policies of West Rise Junior School, where 'forest school' policies accompany the standard curriculum and get excellent results.[30] Let's have Welsh-language education integrated with the rewilding of the land to produce graduates who are physically and mentally healthy from being outdoors, who have craft skills as well as academic knowledge[31] – as well as the cultural skills and confidence they already get from their eisteddfodau. Graduates who know intimately the natural and cultural environment they live in, and who are poised to create local businesses there – in Welsh.

The priority for Wales now is to understand and embrace the changed world that is emerging as 'modernity' dies. Our myths provide inspiration for the responses that are needed: a model of society that draws on the past while integrating the best that can be retained from modernity. We need policies that keep productive land in Welsh-speaking ownership, and we need support for companies to operate entirely in Welsh – including support and assistance to enable people to learn the language so that they can join companies and communities in Welsh.

Inevitably, this will be opposed in some quarters. There will be accusations of 'racism' and 'exclusion'. Here again, our myths provide the response. Those Neolithic people who lost Cantre'r Gwaelod to the sea? They weren't our ancestors. They were almost entirely replaced by Bronze Age settlers[32] – but, like Payn de Turberville, those incomers adopted the language and culture that were already here, becoming Celts and passing on the myths.[33] Our very name for ourselves, Cymry or 'fellow-countrymen', reflects the decision by the warring tribes of Britain to set aside their ethnic hatreds and unite, forging a shared identity in the face of a shared challenge. The Welsh language is not exclusionary; Welshness is an act of participation, not genes, as my own Somerset ancestors found. In a world after 'modernity', and as once happened in the Vale of Glamorgan, Welsh can thrive and spread if it shows that it and its culture are the best avenues to success. Let us be confident that they can be.

ENDNOTES

1 Morris, S. (2022). 'Proportion of Welsh speakers in Wales drops to record low of 17.8%'. *The Guardian.* 7 Dec. https://www.theguardian.com/uk-news/2022/dec/06/proportion-of-welsh-speakers-in-wales-drops-to-record-low-census

2 Encyclopædia Britannica. (n.d.). 'Modernity'. *Britannica Academic.* https://academic.eb.com/levels/collegiate/article/modernity/605418

3 Mackey, A. (2014). 'Language Acquisition' in Fasold, R. W. and Connor-Linton, J. (eds.) *An Introduction to Language and Linguistics.* Cambridge: Cambridge University Press. pp.461–462.

4 This may be a legend. Lots of stories were later invented about Fitzhamon and his knights.

5 (i) Lewis, C. W. (1971). 'The Literary Tradition of Morgannwg Down to the Middle of the Sixteenth Century' in Williams, S. (ed.), *Glamorgan Historian Volume Two.* D. Brown & Sons Limited.

(ii) Smith, J. B. (1971). 'The Kingdom of Morgannwg and the Norman Conquest of Glamorgan', in Pugh, T. B. (ed.), *Glamorgan County History Vol. III: The Middle*

Ages. Cardiff: Glamorgan County History Committee pp.1–44.

6 Davies, J. (2014). *The Welsh Language - A History.* Cardiff: University Of Wales Press p.58.

7 James, B. Ll. (1972). 'The Welsh Language in the Vale of Glamorgan'. *Morgannwg: The Journal of Glamorgan History*, XVI(16–36), p.24.

8 Lindsey, D. T. and Brown, A. M. (2004). 'Sunlight and "Blue": The Prevalence of Poor Lexical Color Discrimination Within the "Grue" Range'. *Psychological Science*, 15(4). p.291.

9 Josserand, M., Meeussen, E., Majid, A. and Dediu, D. (2021). 'Environment and culture shape both the colour lexicon and the genetics of colour perception'. *Scientific Reports*, 11(1). https://doi.org/10.1038/s41598-021-98550-3

10 Weick, K. E. (1995). *Sensemaking in Organizations.* Thousand Oaks, CA: SAGE Publications. p.171.

11 Mintzberg, H., Ahlstrand, B. and Lampel, J. (2009). *Strategy Safari.* 2nd ed. London: Prentice Hall. p.207.

12 Ager, D. (2005). 'Image and Prestige Planning'. *Current Issues in Language Planning*, 6(1), p.7.

13 Jones, R. S. (2011) 'Integrative or instrumental Incentives? Non-Welsh-Speaking Parents and Welsh-Medium Education in the Rhymni Valley, South Wales'. *Journal of Ethnic Studies*, 66. p.57.

14 (i) Wightwick, A. (2023). 'Welsh school put in special measures as children found speaking too much English'. *WalesOnline*. https://www.walesonline.co.uk/news/education/welsh-school-put-special-measures-26147685

(ii) Gruffudd, H. (2000). 'Planning for the Use of Welsh by Young People' in Williams, C. H. (ed.) *Language Revitalization: Policy and Planning in Wales*. Cardiff: University of Wales Press. p.177.

(iii) Jones, R. S. (2011). Op.cit. p.47.

15 (i) Herrington, G. (2021). 'Update to limits to growth: Comparing the World3 model with empirical data'. *Journal of Industrial Ecology*, 25. pp.614–626. https://advisory.kpmg.us/content/dam/advisory/en/pdfs/2021/yale-publication.pdf

(ii) Hall, C. A. S. (2022) 'The 50th Anniversary of The Limits to Growth: Does It Have Relevance for Today's Energy Issues?' *Energies*, 15(14). p.4953. https://canadiancor.com/wp-content/uploads/2022/10/Hall_2022-Limits-to-Growth.pdf

16 Mammadov, R. (2019). 'Could a gas cartel become as powerful as OPEC?' *Middle East Institute*. https://www.mei.edu/publications/could-gas-cartel-become-powerful-opec

17 (i) Kahn, M. (2014). 'The rise of the BRICS and resource nationalism: challenge and opportunity for Africa's innovation systems'. *African Journal of Science, Technology, Innovation and Development*,

6(5): 369–381 https://www.tandfonline.com/doi/full/10 .1080/20421338.2014.970424

(ii) Cobb, K. (2020). 'The Rise Of Resource Nationalism'. oilprice.com https://oilprice.com/Energy/ Energy-General/The-Rise-Of-Resource-Nationalism. html

18 (i) Elliott, L. (2023). 'The AI industrial revolution puts middle-class workers under threat this time'. *The Guardian*. 18 Feb. https://www.theguardian.com/ technology/2023/feb/18/the-ai-industrial-revolution- puts-middle-class-workers-under-threat-this-time

(ii) Yerushalmy, J. (2023). 'German publisher Axel Springer says journalists could be replaced by AI'. *The Guardian*. 1 Mar. https://www.theguardian.com/ technology/2023/mar/01/german-publisher-axel- springer-says-journalists-could-be-replaced-by-ai

19 (i) Morgan Jones, I. (2023). 'Bing AI just wrote me a very entertaining story written in Welsh about a magic hedgehog called Hedydd who took...'. *X* (formerly *Twitter*). 4 Mar. https://twitter.com/ifanmj/ status/1632126510873165825?s=20

(ii) Hughes, Ll. Rh. (2023). 'Chwara têg i Chat GPT!'. Facebook. 16 Mar. https://www. facebook.com/groups/4135170820153371/ permalink/6279610085405978/

20 Schneider, E. W. (2007). *Postcolonial English: Varieties Around the World*. Cambridge: Cambridge University Press. p.315.

21 Nunn, P. (2020). 'In Anticipation of Extirpation: How Ancient Peoples Rationalized and Responded to Postglacial Sea Level Rise'. *Environmental Humanities*, 12(1). pp.113–133.

22 The commonly held belief that the Celts emerged in central Europe is now out of date. Current research shows Celtic culture emerging around the Atlantic seaboard of Neolithic Europe. Cunliffe, B. (2019). 'Setting the Scene' in Cunliffe, B. and Koch, J. T. (eds.) *Exploring Celtic Origins: New ways forward in archaeology, linguistics and genetics*. Oxbow Books. pp.1–17.

23 Nunn, P. (2021). *Worlds in Shadow: Submerged Lands in Science, Memory, and Myth*. London: Bloomsbury Sigma. pp.51–70. There are many interesting articles on his website: https://patricknunn.org/

24 Messenger, S. (2022). 'Farming: Union calls for more help as production costs soar'. *BBC News*. 18 July. https://www.bbc.co.uk/news/uk-wales-62201611

25 van der Zee, B. (2017). 'UK is 30-40 years away from "eradication of soil fertility", warns Gove'. *The Guardian*. https://www.theguardian.com/environment/2017/oct/24/uk-30-40-years-away-eradication-soil-fertility-warns-michael-gove

26 Knepp Estate (n.d.). 'Regenerative Agriculture'. https://knepp.co.uk/knepp-estate/agriculture/regenerative-agriculture/

27   Martynoga, B. (2023). '"The R-word can be alienating":
How Haweswater rewilding project aims to benefit all'.
The Guardian. 10 Mar. https://www.theguardian.com/
environment/2023/mar/10/haweswater-project-lake-
district-rewilding-farming-jobs

28   Daltun, E. (2023). 'A decade ago this was only barren
grasses. Now there's a tangled young species-
rich rainforest, almost every limb adorned with...'.
X (formerly *Twitter*). 2 Mar. https://twitter.com/
IrishRainforest/status/1631172630152638467?s=20

29   Shrubsole, G. (2022). *The Lost Rainforests of
Britain*. London: William Collins Books. pp.95–122.
See also Celtic Rainforests Wales https://
celticrainforests.wales/

30   Pupils help care for water buffalo, learn countryside
and craft skills, and contextualise their academic
studies in their natural and historical environment.

(i) West Rise Junior School. (2023). 'Forest School'.
https://westrisejunior.co.uk/student-projects/forest-
school/

(ii) Fairclough, M. (2016). *Playing with Fire:
Embracing risk and danger in schools*.
Melton: John Catt Educational Ltd.
There are several videos about West Rise Junior
School on *YouTube*.

31   Murphy, M. C. (2020). 'Bronfenbrenner's bio-
ecological model: a theoretical framework to explore
the forest school approach?' *Journal of Outdoor and
Environmental Education*, 23. pp.191–205.

32 Gibson, C. (2019). 'Connectivity in Atlantic Europe' in Cunliffe, B. and Koch, J. T. (eds.) *Exploring Celtic Origins: New ways forward in archaeology, linguistics and genetics.* Oxford: Oxbow Books. p.87.

33 Davis, J. (2021). 'Ancient burials near Stonehenge reveal how cultures merged in the Bronze Age'. *Natural History Museum Science News.* https://www.nhm.ac.uk/discover/news/2021/february/ancient-burials-stonehenge-cultures-merged-in-bronze-age.html

THE FALL OF MÔN

We know from Greek and Roman sources that Anglesey, Ynys Môn, the island separated from North Wales by the narrow, tidal Menai Strait, was the centre of European Druidry: the place where noble youths from across the Celtic world went to study the lore and mysteries of the Druids.

This lasted until AD 60, when Roman troops under Gaius Suetonius Paulinus assaulted the island, destroying the sacred shrines and cutting down the sacred groves. However, Paulinus was called away before he could complete his task, and Druids remained on the island for another seventeen years, until the Romans returned, incorporating it into the Roman province of Britannia.

I myself come from Glamorgan, pretty much as far away from Anglesey as it's possible to be while still being in Wales. I later lived in Aberystwyth, and often travelled up to North Wales. I would go hill-walking on Cadair Idris, Yr Eifl and Yr Wyddfa; I would go surfing at Porth Neigwl at the end of the Llŷn Peninsula. I knew Machynlleth and Dolgellau, Caernarfon and Llanberis, Abersoch and Porthmadog... but I never went to Môn. I didn't imagine it would be anything special.

I was wrong. Môn has something very special about it indeed. Looking south, the great massif of Snowdonia swells up from sea level, rising seemingly vertically in a great black wall. Once you're on Môn, you feel like you're in a self-enclosed world; the rest of the planet seems far, far away.

Much of Môn is low-lying. The mountains of Snowdonia loom over it to the south but, when the air is clear, one can see the mountains of Cumbria to the north-east, lying between Morecambe Bay and the Solway Firth. To the west, the Wicklow Mountains rise high, just south of Dublin. There is a sense of being at the bottom of a great bowl – a cauldron – with the sea around you, the great arch of the sky and stars above you, and walls of rock on all sides. And on Holy Island, just off the west of Môn herself, there rises Holy Mountain, a great natural pulpit, from the summit of which the Druids could observe the skies above and the land and sea spreading out below. Little wonder that this small island is littered with standing stones, burial chambers and other religious markers dating back to the furthest reaches of the past.

Around the shores, sea and land merge and blend; inland there are lakes and rivers that give the same impression. There are oak forests and flowers, and farmland so fertile that over the centuries the Welsh spoke of Môn, Mam Cymru, 'Môn, the mother of Wales', for her ability to produce grain.

Within the cauldron of the Irish Sea floats Môn, self-enclosed, where the elements unite to produce fertility, where the stars are clear and close, where the world is far away. No wonder the Druids decided that this was the ideal place for contemplation, for study, for learning and for education. This was the perfect location for the Druid academy, where students came from all over the Celtic world to be educated – for up to twenty years in some cases, if Caesar is to be believed. Not only did Môn have the tranquillity needed for sustained thought, and the natural environment to stimulate and feed those minds-in-training, it also had the rich lands needed to feed and sustain the academy, all of its staff and students, and the community that would develop around it.

There's one more thing: today, Môn feels remote from the world – but it was actually extremely accessible, because the Celts travelled by sea and Holy Island has a deep-water harbour. The Druids, their students, their warriors and servants would generally not have bothered with the difficult and dangerous struggle through the Welsh mountains unless they were heading inland. For most journeys around Britain, and to the European mainland, they would have gone by sea. It was faster and safer.

The insular Celts used vessels made with wooden frames over which ox-skins or similar materials were stretched and then waterproofed with pitch or oils. These are still used even today. In Wales, they are quite small, used for river fishing; these are known as coracles, which generally only carry one person. In the west of Ireland can be found the currach, which is larger and is used to carry bigger crews out to sea. Though small, the Welsh coracle has been used to cross the English Channel from

England to France, while a currach was used by Tim Severin to travel from Ireland to Newfoundland, recreating the legendary voyage of St Brendan.

In Gaul, we know that the Veneti, who lived in Armorica in the north-west (now known as Brittany), used wooden sailing vessels. These were probably used, amongst other things, to transport people and goods to and from Môn.

Thus, from their port on Holy Island, Druid vessels could very easily reach the entire western coast of Britain, as far as the Pictish kingdom of the Orkneys (it's now accepted that the Picts also spoke British and were a part of the broader Brythonic, Druidic culture). They could reach their colleagues in Gaul, who spoke a similar language, the Gaelic Celts of Ireland and the Gallaeci in north-west Spain. North of the Solway Firth in Britain were the Selgovae; south of them, the Brigantes and the Carvetii. Further north were the Damnonii and the Novantae. From their ports in Môn, Druids could travel to all of the tribes of the North, all of whom acknowledged Druid authority.

It should be understood that during the age of the Druids, the Isle of Man was a British territory, sharing the language and the culture of the mainland. Today, we are used to thinking of the Manx as being part of the Gaelic world, connected to Ireland rather than Britain – but that didn't come about until the post-Roman period. During the days of the Druids, the Manx spoke British.

As a side note, the two smaller islands of the Irish Sea are Manaw (the Isle of Man, masculine form) and Môn

(Mona, feminine form). Was there a sibling myth here that is now lost? Some other relationship? But that's off-topic for the current story...

The Roman conquest of Britain began in 43 AD. It took them a generation to reach Môn, so the Druids had had plenty of time to evaluate the situation, and to make plans. As the Romans advanced, Môn became a place of refuge for Druids and warriors whose own tribal lands had been overrun. These battle-hardened veterans had plenty of knowledge of Roman intentions and methods. They had hopes that the Britons might yet unite and drive the Romans back into the sea. Many would have known Caratacus and learned from his example that guerrilla tactics worked, while set-piece battles did not.

They had time to plan. Lists would have been drawn up of key personnel: the most important Druids, experienced administrators, diplomats, bards, everyone who would be needed to establish a government in exile. A system would have been in place to summon a makeshift fleet, ready to transport those who had been selected to staging camps, probably on Manaw, from where they could move on to the tribes who would give them shelter.

Remember also that the Druids were literate. We tend to forget that their mundane activities were recorded using Greek letters. This means that there would have been large amounts of records: of contacts, trade receipts, administration records. All the documentation of an ancient, Europe-wide organisation. Like any bureaucracy about to fall to an enemy, they would have made sure these records were destroyed, leaving nothing that might endanger allies or benefit the enemy.

The Druids were an ancient order. Seeing Rome's legions slowly advancing towards them across Britain, it's highly unlikely that they would have decided to make a grand, suicidal final stand along the lines of the 1906 Balinese Badung massacre in Denpasar. The Balinese aristocracy had nowhere else to go; the Druids had lines of escape to the northern tribes and a not-unreasonable hope that the Romans might yet be defeated and driven out of Britain, back to Gaul.

So, let's imagine what the scene might have been like when the Romans finally arrived and the evacuation plans were set in motion…

**

After endless days of waiting, days of rumour and tension, messengers arrived with news. Men and horses alike were near death, exhausted from a hard ride through the mountains, pursued by the Romans' cavalry advance guard. They were quickly escorted through our overcrowded island, the villages packed with refugees, to the hall of the Druids. There, they delivered the news: Paulinus and his army would reach Môn within two days at most.

The Archdruid took the news calmly. It had been anticipated for long enough, after all. 'Light the beacon,' he instructed. Men ran through the growing darkness to the peak of Holy Mountain, to summon the evacuation flotilla.

We knew our duties. Across the island, an archipelago of flames slowly spread as our archivists began to destroy that which they had spent their lives preserving: the names of our agents in Gaul, records of diplomatic missions and meetings, even of who had supplied our tools and cloth – best to leave nothing that would allow the Romans to identify our people, or that might be useful to them in any way.

Backlit by those burning papyri and scrolls, long columns of men, women and children shuffled to the port. There, teams of Ovates would check their names against the lists, grouping them for evacuation in order of priority. There was no protest, no fear, no seeking to jump the queue: most had not wished to leave, but the Archdruid, days before, had explained the need. Their knowledge and experience must be preserved so that Druidry could survive, and wait out the Romans in the northern strongholds.

Already, the first were leaving. These were not evacuees. Small groups of horsemen were crossing the strait while it was still open, and into the hills; others were leaving in their coracles, to go down the west coast to the lands of the Ordovices and the Demetae. Some were going to stiffen the resistance of the tribes and strengthen the courage of their warriors. Some would be heading behind enemy lines to set up camps deep in the forests and the marshes, from where they would conduct guerrilla campaigns. And a few, the bravest, were our 'werewolf' units: they would pretend to be farmers and villagers, waging war by night, spreading terror and confusion in the Romans' rear, assassinating collaborators and key officers. It was a suicide mission, and they knew it.

Up until the last moment, we had hoped the Romans would turn around. For weeks, we had been receiving messages that the Iceni, on the other side of Britain, were on the brink of rebellion. If they went to war, Paulinus would be forced to return to fight them; his legionaries would be needed to defend London. But the news never arrived; there were delays, always delays – perhaps the courage of the Iceni had failed...

Finally, the moment came. The Romans marched into view, forming up into ranks on the other side of the strait. On our side, the evacuations continued until the last possible moment, the small boats arriving empty, then leaving again for Manaw with their precious burdens. And those of us not on the lists? We knew there was no way out for us. We knew what our fate would be if – when – the Romans overran us. All that was left for us to do was to delay them for as long as possible and make them pay with much blood for each blasphemous step they took on Môn's sacred soil.

Finally, they came. We put up a fight: all of our Druids, male and female; our warriors; the ordinary tribespeople... We made their soldiers cringe in fear... but eventually, inevitably, their officers restored order. They advanced across the waters – and the killing began.

Killing... and worse. Everyone knows what the Romans do with women. They did it. They immediately began cutting down our sacred groves and destroying our shrines. We kept fighting desperately, retreating further and further back into the marshes and forests as our numbers dwindled.

But they took too long with their sacrilege and their desecration and their raping. Before they had completed their work, more riders came through the mountains – more near-dead men on near-dead horses. Not ours, this time, but theirs. The Iceni had risen at last and were slaughtering the Romans; Paulinus and his men were ordered to leave immediately.

And so, they did... and we, we who survived, emerged back into daylight, back into life to bury our dead, and put out the fires, and to restore the damage to such extent as we could.

Môn was no longer safe. Our exiles could not return now. They would stay in their camps on Manaw until our fleet of small ships could transport them onwards. Those who could speak Irish would move on to the Island of the Blessed. Most would be dispersed among the tribes of the North, a few at each royal court. Our knowledge – the lore and wisdom and honour of the Druids – was secure for the future, but we all knew that an age had come to an end. No longer could our teachers form a college in one place; no longer could they welcome the best minds of Europe, educate them and send them home to their tribes. Our Druids would do their best, but they were diminished.

And we, we left amongst the ruins and graves of Môn, began to plan for the future – for a new age – when the Druids could return.

STOPPING THE ROT

Corruption is a mortal threat, and I'm getting worried.

The journalist Negley Farson[1] lived an exceedingly full life. Among many other adventures between the wars, he and his wife Eve (niece of *Dracula* author Bram Stoker) lived on a houseboat on a lake on Vancouver Island; sailed a narrowboat across Europe, from Holland to the Black Sea; and drove across Africa from east to west.

As a young man, Farson worked in marketing. When the First World War broke out, this experience got him hired by American industrialists to sell vehicles and other war materials to the Tsarist government. He describes his time in the Russian capital, Saint Petersburg, in his memoir, *The Way of a Transgressor*, in which he describes an environment of uncontrolled corruption. Even submitting a proposal to the authorities required paying 'fixers' who had the right connections. Getting a contract signed involved huge kickbacks and, once the goods finally arrived at a Russian port, yet more bribes had to be paid for them to be transported to where they were needed.

The same was true domestically. Vast quantities of produce rotted in warehouses and railway sidings while bribes were negotiated or not paid. The food and winter fuel that did reach the cities was hoarded, to be sold on the black market.

The population starved and shivered while its men died in droves at the front for lack of equipment. They sullenly endured, putting up with it all until, one day, they didn't. The anger couldn't be contained anymore. Revolution erupted, overthrowing and erasing a regime that had lost its legitimacy.

A similar dynamic played out in China. The Guomindang government and state were so unashamedly corrupt, on such a vast scale, that it drove the bulk of the people to support the communists, leading to Mao's victory in 1949. The discipline and incorruptibility of the Party and the People's Liberation Army were widely admired at the time.

This had consequences elsewhere. Throughout south-east Asia, national liberation movements led to post-WWII independence from their colonial masters – and a rapid descent into spectacular corruption, fuelling communist insurgencies and guerrilla wars. As in China, the incorruptibility of the communists was a leading reason for their ultimate victory in Vietnam.

Corruption corrodes state legitimacy from the inside. There may be warning signs before it collapses. There may not.

The sense of corruption now pervades the British state – I've got a word limit here, so I won't try to list examples. If you're reading this, you're already interested enough in politics to know that, wherever we turn, they seem dominated by financial interests, not the interests of the people. Regardless of the details, regardless of whether rules are broken, we get the feeling that money talks and voting won't change much. Sullen discontent is simmering. All around, we hear that Britain is broken.[2]

And that's dangerous.

Are there signs that the system is breaking down? They're staring us in the face. Violence, intimidation and abuse mean that good people simply don't want to stand for election, even at the local level.[3] Those who do stand and are elected have to be given a guidebook on how to handle intimidation.[4] Even in Westminster, the level of threats to MPs' personal safety[5] is becoming intolerable,[6] causing some to step down who might have served longer. The democratic system is being hollowed out.

Meanwhile, on the ground, the destruction of cameras in London's ULEZ area by so-called 'blade runners'[7] has been met by a collective shrug, it seems, even when it involved the use of explosives.[8] Wales isn't immune to this, with road signs being defaced or destroyed across the country[9] and a government minister driven off X by the level of abuse.[10] Disillusion undermines devolution.

All of these are indications that civil society is breaking down, and that government at all levels is losing its legitimacy. We shouldn't underestimate the danger of this, because the disillusionment, the social corrosion, will only spread if its cause is not addressed.

The system no longer works. Violence, verbal or physical, is undermining the vote. Can this genie be put back in the bottle?

I can't see how it can be done for Westminster, and that's one of the reasons why the United Kingdom can't be saved. Research by the think tank Onward (which is explicitly aligned with the Conservative Party, so bear that in mind) finds that 25% of young people have lost faith in democracy, with an even higher percentage amongst the non-university-educated and those who are economically worse-off.[11] These are the people whose voice is least likely to be heard by those in power. It's also the demographic that historically sparks and supports revolutions – which are then hijacked by disillusioned intellectuals.[12]

The independence movement in Wales needs to address this. If it can make itself clean, disciplined and legitimate, it stands to gain a huge boost in support. But can it? It'll be an uphill struggle, I fear. Unfortunately, all of the parties seem to have settled into complacency, giving the impression that they're really just more of the same. This is feeding the sense of democratic failure.

It's not too late, though. Welsh politics is small enough and, I still believe, idealistic enough to turn this around.

According to the anti-corruption NGO Transparency International, the top five most honest states in the world in 2023 were Denmark, Finland, New Zealand, Norway and Singapore. The UK was twentieth out of 180.[13] All of the top five are small countries, and the first four are relatively homogenous – or were so until quite recently – with strong national identities and community ethos.

The exception is Singapore, which had to turn around an existing culture of corruption and political disengagement.

They did so by setting up an independent Corrupt Practices Investigation Bureau, which has 'a fearsome and trusted reputation'[14] for its pitiless enforcement of extremely strict anti-corruption legislation, willing and able to arrest even cabinet ministers.[15] Public officials are highly paid, to attract the best talent; donations to political parties and individual politicians are very tightly regulated, particularly those from overseas.[16]

Let's take Singapore as a model. Modify its anti-corruption laws for Wales if necessary. Then let's see Gwlad, the Greens, Plaid Cymru, the Liberal Democrats and Labour for Indy publicly commit to meeting these standards and making them law on independence day – or even before then, if the devolution settlement allows. Let's have a rigorous cross-party, anti-corruption charter. No need to wait: it could be done today. Those who won't sign must be made to explain why.

The corruption of Westminster is destroying its moral authority. In Wales, we still have the opportunity to shore up and preserve clean politics and democratic legitimacy if we act quickly. If we don't take this opportunity, we will reap the whirlwind as the disillusioned turn elsewhere: to the far right or, worse, those who don't believe in democracy at all.

The window of opportunity may be smaller than we think. A black swan event, something like a serious royal scandal or the unexpected loss of the Falklands,[17] could precipitate a major political crisis, and then all bets will be off.

There's no time to lose. Let the sunshine in.

ENDNOTES

1   Bram Stoker Estate. (n.d.). 'James Scott Negley Farson'. https://www.bramstokerestate.com/james-scott-negley-farson

2   (i) Kellner, P. (2023). 'Who Will Repair Broken Britain?' *Carnegie Europe*. https://carnegieeurope.eu/strategiceurope/88917

   (ii) Monbiot, G. (2023). 'Britain is broken. What will fix it? Lots and lots of money'. *The Guardian*. 22 Nov. https://www.theguardian.com/commentisfree/2023/nov/22/britain-money-bank-bailouts-state-failure.

   (iii) Lansley, S. (2023). 'Broken Britain and the return of "private affluence and public squalor"'. British Politics and Policy at *LSE*. 22 Sep. https://blogs.lse.ac.uk/politicsandpolicy/broken-britain-and-the-return-of-private-affluence-and-public-squalor/

3   Haynes, C. (2024). 'Abuse of councillors and staff putting democracy at risk, say local government groups'. *BBC News*. 5 Feb. https://www.bbc.co.uk/news/uk-politics-68167190

4   Councillors' guide to handling intimidation. (n.d.). https://www.local.gov.uk/sites/default/files/

documents/Full%20word%20english%20version%20 guide%20for%20councillors%20on%20handling%20 intimidation_FINAL.pdf

5   Creasy, S. (2024). 'Death and rape threats, bricks through windows: MPs must be able to serve without living in fear'. *The Guardian*. 22 Feb. https://www. theguardian.com/commentisfree/2024/feb/22/death-threats-mps-politicians-protesters

6   Morton, B. (2024). '£31m package announced to counter threat to MPs' security'. *BBC News*. 28 Feb. https://www.bbc.co.uk/news/uk-politics-68419987

7   Sayce, R. (2023). 'Who are the ULEZ Blade Runners? Story behind the camera vandals'. *Metro*. https:// metro.co.uk/2023/08/01/ulez-blade-runners-london-camera-vandals-19228527/

8   Bugel, S. (2023).' Counter-terrorism arrests after Ulez camera blown up in London'. *The Guardian*. 18 Dec. https://www.theguardian.com/uk-news/2023/dec/18/ counter-terrorism-police-arrest-two-men-after-ulez-camera-blown-up-in-south-east-london

9   (i) Evans, T. (2024). '20mph sign "removed illegally" amid "spate of incidents" in Welsh village'. *Sky News*. https:// news.sky.com/story/20mph-sign-removed-illegally-amid-spate-of-incidents-in-welsh-village-13088570

(ii) Forgrave, A. (2023). 'Police action warning as 20mph road signs torn down and defaced'. *North Wales Live*. https://www.dailypost.co.uk/news/north-wales-news/police-action-warning-20mph-road-27754661

10 Price, E. (2023). 'Welsh Govt minister to take break from social media following torrent of online abuse'. Nation.Cymru. https://nation.cymru/news/welsh-govt-minister-to-take-break-from-social-media-following-torrent-of-online-abuse/

11 Lennard, N. (2018). 'The Kids Aren't Alright'. *Dissent*, 65(1). pp.132–134. https://doi.org/10.1353/dss.2018.0003

12 Lawford, M. (2023). 'The ticking time bomb under Britain's universities'. *The Telegraph*. 17 Dec. https://www.telegraph.co.uk/business/2023/12/17/british-university-finances-ticking-time-bomb/

13 Transparency International (2024). '2023 Corruption Perceptions Index – Explore United Kingdom's Results'. Transparency.org. https://www.transparency.org/en/cpi/2023/index/gbr

14 (i) CPIB (2021). 'Corruption Situation In Singapore'. www.cpib.gov.sg. https://www.cpib.gov.sg/press-room/press-releases/corruption-situation-singapore/

(ii) CPIB (2023). 'Singapore's Corruption Control Framework'. www.cpib.gov.sg. https://www.cpib.gov.sg/about-corruption/prevention-and-corruption/singapores-corruption-control-framework/

15 Agence France-Presse (2023). 'Singapore arrests cabinet minister in top-level corruption probe'. *The Guardian*. 15 Jul. https://www.theguardian.com/world/2023/jul/15/singapore-arrests-cabinet-minister-in-top-level-corruption-probe

16   Elections Department Singapore (n.d.). 'Overview of Political Donations Act'. www.eld.gov.sg. https://www.eld.gov.sg/registry.html

17   (i) Conway, E. (2024). 'Argentinian President Javier Milei says he has begun discussions with UK about Falkland Islands'. *Sky News*. https://news.sky.com/story/argentinian-president-javier-milei-says-he-has-begun-discussions-with-uk-about-falkland-islands-13050472

(ii) Diver, T. (2024). 'Royal Navy scraps major warship patrols around the Falklands'. *The Telegraph*. 2 Feb. https://www.telegraph.co.uk/world-news/2024/02/02/falkland-islands-royal-navy-warship-patrols-javier-milei/

THE GROANS OF THE WELSH

In 1926, the literary and political icon Saunders Lewis argued that Wales needed to focus on developing its own distinct civilisation rather than on independence. As part of that, he called for the complete deindustrialisation of South Wales. That must have sounded preposterous at the time, and Lewis's contemporaries focused instead on the political struggle. And yet, just short of a century later, Lewis has been vindicated. Wales is still not independent but it has indeed experienced deindustrialisation. In the meantime, Welsh thinkers adopted a model developed by Michael Hechter and popularised by Gwynfor Evans: Wales as a colony of England. It remains a useful framework as we experience intense global change, because it helps us to understand that we've faced collapse before – and we can learn important lessons from that.

Sometime around 450 AD, the leaders of Roman Britain sent a desperate appeal for assistance – the 'Groans of the Britons' – to Flavius Aetius, commander of imperial forces in Europe. Britain was being assaulted by barbarian raiders, but the last legions had been withdrawn to the continent decades earlier. Aetius couldn't help them:

the Roman Empire in the west was collapsing, overrun by nomadic Huns and German tribes. The emperor, Valentian III, could only try to stem the chaos and restore some temporary stability. Imperial resources were at breaking point, and Britain wasn't worth the investment needed to keep it. Aetius replied that the Britons were on their own and must organise their own defence. Their centuries of living as part of a vast empire were over. From now on they would have to depend on whatever skills and resources they had locally.

The Age of Arthur had begun. Unable to cooperate and weakened by internal struggles, the Britons lost their lands until, finally, they united and became the Cymry, hanging on in the west. As Rome's vast factories and open trade routes faded into history, the Welsh wouldn't have a standard of living equal to that of their Romano-British ancestors for many, many centuries.

History moves in cycles. Empires and civilisations rise, fall, and sometimes rise again in a new form. Languages and cultures ebb and flow. Nothing has a right to endure for ever. We're once again at the end of a cycle of history, and on the cusp of another.

The industrialisation of Wales is comparatively recent in historical terms. It created an entirely new, English-speaking society on foundations of coal and steel: one that has existed now for about the same length of time as the Tudor dynasty. The Tudors died out. The coal industry vanished decades ago, and today, with the steelworks in Port Talbot soon to close, we are seeing the end of an economy that began in the late eighteenth century but only really took its modern form in the nineteenth. Without coal and steel, what future does Anglo-Welsh society have? The trends since the 1980s aren't encouraging.

We need to ask these difficult questions and come up with answers very quickly now. It seems that when the news about Port Talbot broke, Mark Drakeford tried to speak to Rishi Sunak – and was curtly informed that the Prime Minister was not available. Aetius at least wrote back to the Britons.

Comparing the Rome of 450 AD to today's United Kingdom is useful because Britain is still an imperial system in many ways. The Industrial Revolution which created the coal and steel communities was also the launchpad for Europe's empires. As our own mineral reserves were depleted, we used materials from the colonies – obtained cheaply because we could impose the terms – to keep our industries going. Even after those colonies became politically independent, the old imperial centres remained economically dominant and the relationship extractive.

That's changing, though, as ancient civilisations rise again. For most of history, China, India and Persia (Iran) were the most powerful and wealthy parts of the world. Today, we see them resuming this historical role, joined by Russia as a new Eurasian power, and collaborating via partnerships such as the BRICS. As they rise, other nations are gravitating towards their diplomatic and economic influence – not least because they think they can get a better deal than the West has given them, as recent events in west and central Africa show.

Economies need raw materials, and they need energy. The UK is now in trouble on both fronts. Booming economies in the Global South are increasing demand and pushing up prices. Producer nations are demanding fair compensation for their commodities and, increasingly, keeping processing (such as steel production) for themselves, increasing prices even more. Worse, the global reserves of the most important resources, particularly oil, are in decline; it's now believed that global demand for oil will permanently outstrip supply from 2025 onwards: that's next year. Prices will reach previously unimaginable levels, which is very bad news for the energy-intensive economy of the UK as its North Sea reserves decline. Already, the cost of energy is collapsing industrial production in the former European powerhouses of Germany and Italy.

The signs are that this is causing panic in Westminster. The former Secretary General of NATO, George Robertson, warns that the West must overcome Russia to maintain dominance over the world order. Energy Secretary Claire Coutinho fears that once the UK depends on energy bought from overseas it will become 'subservient to foreign regimes'. Brexit negotiator Lord Frost declares that London must maintain its rule over Wales and Scotland or face 'massive national humiliation'.

This all means very hard times to come for Wales. London will do everything it can to keep control; it needs our water and our potential for renewable energy. We should expect further efforts to undermine devolution and such political autonomy as we have, and we must understand that all available resources will be reserved for the imperial core, even as the cost of living escalates beyond our worst nightmares.

Think of the funds taken for HS2, and the refusal to fund work on hundreds of unsafe coal tips. We can expect London to engage in ever more desperate military adventures to look strong, even as the UK's armed forces collapse in size and strength.

The Welsh must understand that we stand alone, that the way of life we are used to has gone forever – and that we will only survive if we unite and face the reality of our situation with clear eyes and no illusions. Aetius and his legions are not coming to help us. Nor are outside investors, multinational corporations – or Westminster.

For two generations we've lived in a global, borderless economy which brought us cheap goods, cheap energy and cheap food. That time is over. We need to accept it and deal with it, just as the citizens of Britannia had to accept that Rome had cut them loose. As Wales loses its industry, and our communities lose their economic reasons to exist, we must stop reacting to events. Rather, we must establish a clear image of who we want to be as a nation and be single-minded – united – in creating it ourselves. Nobody is coming to help us. It's up to us now.

LOSING A WELSH IDENTITY

Are we losing a Welsh identity, I wonder? There are good reasons to think we might be.

I recently read a post on X about predicted election results in the new parliamentary constituency of Merthyr Tydfil and Aberdare.[1] The connected report indicates a Labour victory, with the Reform party coming second and Plaid Cymru third. Reform are credited with just under a fifth of the vote. 'How could this be,' the anonymous poster asked, 'when Reform's policies have little connection to Wales?'

Martin Shipton, writing for nation.cymru, offers an explanation: voters are fed up with the Conservative government but are uninspired by Keir Starmer's Labour party, which isn't really offering anything beyond a change of faces.[2] Voters, Shipton suggests, are therefore increasingly turning to populist right-wing parties such as Reform, which are perceived as addressing their concerns rather than those of big business.

While I suspect this is probably true, it's only a part of the answer – at least in Wales. Here, I think we are going to see a substantial growth in support for these parties as a consequence of the death throes of Anglo-Welsh culture.

When I say we are 'losing a Welsh identity', then, I mean one of them. For decades, the two identities of Wales – Welsh-speaking and English-speaking – have lived alongside each other in an often uneasy relationship which has generated many articles, books and even TV productions.

These discussions have usually focused primarily on the language, particularly as the Welsh language declined in terms of the percentage of people in Wales who speak it, the number of communities where it was the primary language, and in total numbers.

Welsh is, of course, the ancient and original language of Wales. English-speaking Wales has always been insecure about this. There's very much been a current of self-justification: of having to argue that the Anglo-Welsh are just as Welsh as the Cymry Cymraeg. And, of course, the Anglo-Welsh are far and away the majority of the population.

What does it mean to be Anglo-Welsh, though? Culture is far more than just language. Culture is what enables us to survive in a particular environment. It covers everything from who and what we value and respect to the formal and informal rules for formal and informal interactions, as well as the shared experiences that bind us together as part of a group – and that make us different from other groups. Culture is the difference between 'us' and 'them'.

In Wales, many of these things crossed the language boundary: rugby, football, cricket. The chapels. Working down the pits or in the steelworks. All these things bound the two communities together and, with institutions like the male voice choirs, made Wales and its two identities distinctive, and different from the rest of the United Kingdom. Just watching the classic 1978 TV movie *Grand Slam* illustrates this, featuring as it does members of a rugby club from South Wales flying to Paris to watch a rugby match. Although the characters are Anglo-Welsh, the Welsh language is threaded through the dialogue, reflecting the bilingual nature of many industrial communities.

Indeed, the writer and poet Robert Graves, who served with the Royal Welch Fusiliers in WWI, declared in the 1920s that the Welsh were being transformed into a new people whose culture hero was the collier.

This environment has changed, though. The chapels, pits and now steelworks are all gone. The sports are increasingly emphasising the Welsh language. The collier has long since left the Welsh scene. What's left for those who don't speak Welsh and don't want to?

The existence of the English-speaking communities is, in historical terms, a very recent development. The industrial communities were originally mostly Welsh in their language, and it was only at the beginning of the twentieth century that English became the majority tongue. This new community lacked a name; it was only in the 1920s that Idris Bell coined 'Anglo-Welsh' for the new culture that was just emerging.

Most of the wealth that Wales produced left across Offa's Dyke, but enough remained to sustain a new literary and cultural identity in English. Local newspapers in Welsh communities acted as the foundation on which authors such as Dylan Thomas, Raymond Garlick, Danny Absie and others could build literary careers. The arrival of radio and the BBC – also in the 1920s – provided another arena in which the Anglo-Welsh could recognise themselves and develop cultural figures.

All of these things provided shared cultural references that were familiar to large numbers of people, establishing the English-speakers of Wales as different from those in England.

However, these things are now joining the coal mines in the rear-view mirror. Many Welsh-based news sources have been amalgamated or closed, and those that remain are increasingly owned by multinational corporations who don't keep many local reporters. The Anglo-Welsh literary scene is collapsing as well, with the closure of the *New Welsh Review* and *Planet: The Welsh Internationalist* just the latest blows.

This isn't to suggest that Welsh-language culture isn't also experiencing a crisis – it is – but the Cymry Cymraeg have an ancient history. They aren't defined by a particular historical moment as the Anglo-Welsh are and that, I think, gives them more resilience.

The Anglo-Welsh, in contrast, are losing most of what defines them as a distinct cultural group. They will, no doubt, continue to be the largest group that defines itself as 'Welsh only' on the census. The figures for 'Welsh and British' are creeping up, though, and I would suggest that this is what will become the dominant mindset, whatever the census returns say. They may still sing 'Delilah', but that was released in 1967, in a Wales that's now gone and which many of us never knew.

As the amount of 'Welsh' content in Anglo-Welsh culture diminishes, the 'Anglo' element will increase. Not so much that of England, but of the transnational, transatlantic Anglosphere consumed online. Not American, not English, and increasingly insecure about their Welshness compared to the Cymry, more and more Anglo-Welsh will reach for 'Britishness' and the Union to secure their identity.

This cultural decay is probably invisible to the political classes and commentariat in Cardiff Bay. It's manifesting first amongst the former working class and the precariat – but it will spread further.

And this, I suggest, is why parties such as Reform will flourish. This sector of the electorate will never vote for Plaid Cymru. Welsh Labour is too complicit in 'forcing Welsh down their throats', and the Conservatives are historically too repugnant for any Valleys community, even without their recent descent into 'blanket 20mph' buffoonery. So, who can they turn to? The new populism, which has no such baggage and champions the 'Britishness' that has traditionally provided comfort to a community with very shallow historical roots.

With the Welsh government seemingly unable to restore any prosperity to these communities, and seemingly 'at war'[3] with anything that would restore a cultural distinctiveness, this is a trend that will only grow. Expect to see the vote for Reform and its ilk – and for undoing devolution – grow as the Anglo-Welsh identity fades away.

ENDNOTES

1   Polling Report (n.d.). 'Merthyr Tydfil and Aberdare | W07000099'. pollingreport.uk. https://pollingreport.uk/seats/W07000099

2   Mansfield, M. (2024). 'Labour must improve its offer to the people – or hard right populists will seize the agenda'. Nation.Cymru. https://nation.cymru/opinion/labour-must-improve-its-offer-to-the-people-or-hard-right-populists-will-seize-the-agenda/

3   Green, A. (2024). 'Is the Welsh Government at war with arts, culture, and heritage?' *Bylines Cymru*. https://bylines.cymru/arts-and-culture/heritage-culture-arts/

THE WORLD NEEDS WELSH CULTURAL INTELLIGENCE

Right now, there's a huge opportunity for Wales to increase its international profile. It's ready for the taking. All we need to do is turn the Druidic vision of the eighteenth-century Welsh polymath and poetic genius Iolo Morganwg into reality.

'Cultural intelligence' – the ability to communicate and work effectively across cultures – is a booming field these days. It's critical in a global economy, because it turns out that people aren't actually the same wherever they are. They think in different ways, they perceive the world in different ways, and they value very different things. An important centre of research in this field is Singapore's Nanyang Business School (NBS), with its Cultural Quotient (CQ) framework.[1] Singapore is a natural place for this, given its multicultural population, its location in incredibly diverse south-east Asia and its role as a hub for multinational businesses.

Since human behaviour and cognition can't be reduced to one model, though, there are others besides CQ. One is Geert Hofstede's system of Cultural Dimensions,[2] which models societies using the metrics of Power Distance, Short-term vs Long-term Thinking, Masculinity vs Femininity, Individual vs Collective Identity, Indulgence vs Restraint, and Tolerance for Uncertainty.[3]

Another important framework was developed by Terrence Deal and Allan Kennedy.[4] Although originally intended to describe the internal culture of organisations, it's very applicable to national cultures. In this context, the model evaluates a given group's shared history, its values and beliefs, its shared rituals and ceremonies, the stories that members tell each other, the heroes it reveres and the nature of its internal networks.

Wales, for example, regards itself as being more collectivist that England – but is that because of industrial-era class solidarity or the somewhat older shared history of being a clan-based society?

All of these factors combine to form connections between words, phrases, cultural references and emotional responses in what are called 'semantic maps'.[5] Take the question: 'Is there peace?' If you're monoglot English, I can't predict what will come into your mind in response. I suspect, though, that Welsh-speakers would immediately interpret it as 'A oes heddwch?' – the question demanded of the audience by the Archdruid during the ceremony of the Chairing of the Bard at the annual National Eisteddfod of Wales. Without prompting, their mind's eye will see the assembled Bards, Ovates and Druids in their different-coloured robes, the Grand Sword which is never unsheathed, and the singing of the Druid's Prayer. They'll automatically associate it with culture heroes such as tragic Hedd Wyn, and with their personal networks connected to Eisteddfod-going. Of course, each individual's emotional response will be influenced by their personal experience of the Eisteddfod, because all semantic maps are ultimately personal, but having this kind of foundational, shared 'map of meanings' is essential for a coherent, functional society.

In *Barddas*, Iolo describes the Bard's role:

The three principal endeavours of a Bard: one is to learn and collect sciences; the second is to teach; and the third is to make peace, and to put an end to all injury[.]

In Iolo's model, a Bard is not simply a poet: his or her knowledge of language and science is to be used to bring peace. Iolo builds on Julius Caesar's account to assert that experienced Bards became Druids, and it was they who formed 'the Gorsedd of judgment and judicature', which possessed the special right to determine national and social disputes.

I don't know how many Druids there are in Strasbourg, but the Council of Europe (CoE), which is based there, recently updated its Common European Framework of References for Languages (CEFR).[6] This is an internationally adopted model for measuring someone's ability in a language, which traditionally was assessed on one's command of grammar and vocabulary in the four fields of speaking, listening, reading and writing. With the growth of globalisation and multiculturalism, the CoE recognised that this was no longer sufficient and, in 2020, revised the CEFR to include mediation skills. This addition requires speakers at higher levels of ability to demonstrate, essentially, that they can grasp the semantic maps that are influencing the use of language by people from other cultures, and use that understanding to translate the intended meaning into a form appropriate to their own semantic map (and vice versa). These are core skills for interpreters and translators and are exactly the skill set that Iolo Morganwg required for his Bards and Druids. They are also seen in the requirements of the International Mediation Institute, based in The Hague, which recognises that such translingual and transcultural mediation skills are needed to arbitrate and resolve international disputes.

This is precisely where a huge opportunity is waiting for Wales.

Our Welsh-medium schools are, by default, bilingual and bicultural. If they are assessing their pupils' language ability on the updated 2020 CEFR scale (and they should be), then every single young person emerging from our schools should be trained in cross-language and cross-cultural mediation. The example above – evaluating why Welsh-speakers and English-speakers have different responses to 'Is there peace?' – shows just how easy it is to introduce cultural intelligence skills into the classroom. What's more, every single pupil should be taught dispute-resolution mediation. The method for doing this is fully-formed and ready to use: the Peer Mediation Network have been training schoolchildren to resolve disputes for years.[7] This model needs to be adopted and integrated into the Welsh education system.

And why stop there? Let's make Wales an international centre of excellence for intercultural mediation. I propose that such a centre be established in the Vale of Glamorgan – partly to honour Iolo Morganwg, who lived there, but also because it's close to both the School of Culture and Communication at Swansea University, with their specialism in interpreting and translation, and to Atlantic College: an international sixth-form college founded explicitly to promote international peace and understanding, whose insights and contributions would be invaluable. The centre would be able to draw on the experience of Wales-based Cymdeithas y Cymod[8] and would model itself on the Singapore Mediation Centre, using the world-class Singapore Convention on Mediation. [9]

Two millennia ago, Caesar wrote that the Druids of Gaul held an annual festival at which they would hear and resolve disputes. Let modern Wales hold an annual winter festival of mediation, inviting disputants from around the world to attend and, with the assistance of Welsh experts, find resolution. In this way, Wales will bring the nations of the world together in summer song at Llangollen in the north and, in winter, resolve their disputes in the south.

We can establish Wales on the world stage as an international leader in peace and reconciliation. It would be easy to achieve, and we're a natural place for it: mediation is a part of our history and – thanks to Iolo – ingrained in our national culture. All we have to do is keep on doing what we already are, with a bit more funding, a bit more focus and some motivated planning. Amdani! Let's go for it!

(Full disclosure: I took my MBA degree at Nanyang Business School and am a certified mediator with the

International Mediation Institute. I attended Atlantic College on a full scholarship from South Glamorgan County Council.)

ENDNOTES

1   Pogosyan, M. (2022). 'The What, How and Why of Cultural Intelligence'. *Psychology Today*. 29 Jun. https://www.psychologytoday.com/us/blog/between-cultures/202206/the-what-how-and-why-cultural-intelligence

2   Nickerson, C. (2023). 'Hofstede's Cultural Dimensions Theory & Examples'. *Simply Psychology*. https://www.simplypsychology.org/hofstedes-cultural-dimensions-theory.html

3   Hofstede Insights (2024). 'Country Comparison Tool'. *The Culture Factor*. https://www.hofstede-insights.com/country-comparison-tool

4   Mind Tools Content Team (n.d.). 'MindTools | Home'. www.mindtools.com. https://www.mindtools.com/avnhbho/deal-and-kennedys-cultural-model

5   Georgakopoulos, T. (2019). 'Semantic Maps'. *Oxford Bibliographies*. https://www.oxfordbibliographies.com/display/document/obo-9780199772810/obo-9780199772810-0229.xml

6   Council of Europe (n.d.). *Common European Framework of Reference for Languages (CEFR)*.

www.coe.int. https://www.coe.int/en/web/common-european-framework-reference-languages/

[7] Peer Mediation Network (n.d.). 'HOME'. https://www.peermediationnetwork.org.uk/

[8] Cymdeithas y Cymod. (n.d.). 'Home'. https://www.cymdeithasycymod.cymru/en/home/

[9] (i) Singapore Mediation Centre (n.d.). 'Singapore Mediation Centre'. mediation.com.sg. https://mediation.com.sg/about-us/about-smc/

(ii) Singapore International Dispute Resolution Academy (2021). 'Home | Singapore Convention on Mediation'. https://www.singaporeconvention.org/

SENSE-MAKING IN SLEBECH

Facts are slippery things. The best are repeatable, evidence-based and attested to by reliable people. Many are taken on faith, or on the word of people who prove fallible. Either way, facts are infinite. If we tried to take all facts into account, we wouldn't be able to decide anything: we'd be overwhelmed. We have to select those we deem relevant and make a judgement call.

Sometimes, the facts are uncertain; sometimes, there are none available. We have to fill the gaps with conjecture. Thus, we move from description to narrative to myth. So when I say that Slebech was where Owain Glyndŵr took his last steps on Welsh soil, I'm myth-building, constructing a sense-making narrative from the best facts available to me.

I'm standing in a green chapel: the ancient church of Slebech. Grass and soft moss cover the floor where worshippers once gathered. The walls lead up to open sky, and the only hymns this morning are sung by massed choirs of birds. A mutilated font stands in the south-east, filled with fallen leaves and rainwater. It hasn't seen a baptism for centuries. The crumbling window arches hold no glass. In the north-west, a simple wooden cross overlooks the tidal Cleddau Ddu river, where a ship once waited for Glyndŵr to finish his prayers before embarking for the East.

Where's Slebech, you ask? Some will know it as a blink-and-you'll-miss-it hamlet in Pembrokeshire, on the A40 from London to Fishguard and the ferry to Rosslare. Turn off the main road, though, and you'll find a magical place: Slebech Park Estate, a hotel in what was once one of the most important places in Wales.[1] Today, it's fallen into obscurity. 'Nobody knows we're here,' says one of the staff ruefully.

This was the west Wales headquarters of the Order of Knights of the Hospital of St John of Jerusalem: the Hospitallers. They were warrior monks, a military order established in 1099 to protect pilgrims travelling to the Holy Land. They swore their allegiance to Christ embodied in the poor, not to any worldly leader. Their mission was to provide shelter, food and medical care to the poor and needy, regardless of faith; Christian, Jew or Muslim, all received Hospitaller protection. (Suppressed in Britain by Henry VIII, their legacy survives in the St John Ambulance Brigade.) Slebech was one of their more important British bases.

By the time Glyndŵr was born in the mid-fourteenth century, the order was struggling. Driven out of the Holy Land, they were now based on the island of Rhodes. From here, apart from their original mission, the brother knights (of noble birth) and brother sergeants (commoners) were engaged in defending the Christian kingdoms of the eastern Mediterranean against the forces of Islam.

Glorious camellias with abundant pink flowers stand below the church's broken, ivy-wrapped tower on this February morning. As I listen to the tapping of a distant woodpecker in the stillness and watch the early-morning mist rise from the river, it truly feels like a place of refuge.

The Hospitallers also served pilgrims in Wales. Slebech was an important stop on the way to St David's, to which two pilgrimages equalled one to Rome.[2] From here, they managed pilgrim hospices in bandit-infested mid-Wales. These were badly run-down in Glyndŵr's time. The need to support their work in the East meant that all available resources – including their substantial Welsh revenues – were sent there. Very little was invested locally.

Glyndŵr and the Hospitallers almost certainly knew each other. Hospitaller estates in North Wales, including Ysbyty Ifan, were managed from Halston Hall in Shropshire, just a few miles from Glyndŵr's home at Sycharth.[3] Halston was probably the 'Nillystan Trevan' – 'a sanctuary from time immemorial'[4] – in *Rhonabwy's Dream* (written down in Glyndŵr's lifetime for his ally, the soldier-seer Hopcyn ap Thomas ab Einion). The Hospitallers did indeed have the right to give sanctuary to fugitives.[5]

We have no known facts about Glyndŵr's later years, but we can conjecture. His rebellion was petering out by 1412, when he was last reliably seen. He had lost his lands and strongholds; his army was defeated and dwindling. What would a reasonable man do? Surrender, and accept Henry V's offer of a pardon? Too humiliating. Fight on? That would risk being captured alive and perhaps an excruciating, shameful traitor's death. Flee to France, like Owain Lawgoch in an earlier generation? Too uncertain, with Henry already claiming the French throne. Perhaps go into hiding with his Scudamore in-laws in Herefordshire? Again, risky, should the political winds change. Anyway, Glyndŵr was still in his prime, and nobles of that period were often active well into their eighties. Hiding would mean decades of isolation, boredom and inactivity for a man who had ruled a nation and commanded armies.

There was, though, a solution: to join the Hospitallers as a brother knight. The order had an unquestionable right to give him sanctuary. He knew them of old as a neighbour and as a prince. They wouldn't have cared that he was a rebel; their only thought would be that, as a Christian Prince of Wales, he hadn't interrupted their work. Indeed, they would have enthusiastically welcomed him. In 1402, while Glyndŵr's rebellion was gathering momentum, the Hospitallers had suffered a massive defeat when their stronghold of Smyrna was overrun by the armies of Timur, Emperor of Central Asia, whose capital was in distant Samarkand.[6] The brothers' main redoubt was now Bodrum, in modern Türkiye, and they were desperately short of fighting men. Glyndŵr's skills and experience would have been urgently needed.

So perhaps he rode with a party of his new brother monks through Wales to Slebech. Tonsured, clean-shaven and wearing black Hospitaller robes, he would have been unrecognisable. From Slebech, he would have left Wales with the ebbing tide, away to Asia and beyond the reach of English revenge. His rebellion had failed, but he could still die with honour as a soldier of Christ – or of old age, in the care of his fellow warrior-monks. Even better, his son Maredudd could then accept Henry's pardon and live freely – which he did in 1421.

Did it happen this way? It fits the known facts as well as any other account. It's plausible – and it's more inspiring. Owain Glyndŵr, rebel Prince of Wales, got away in the end and died with honour in Asia.

What of Slebech? The fact is that, for four centuries, much of the wealth of Wales was exported from here. How we interpret this, though, is up to us. It's tempting to say that it's just another example of our long history of being exploited. Or we could be positive, acknowledging that the Welsh were as pious as any other nation in Christendom and that, through Slebech, they played their part in a pan-European endeavour. Not one of conquest, but of sustaining poor and weak pilgrims of all nations and all faiths. Which is preferable?

Facts are useful, but a sense-making narrative is everything. If, today, the facts about Wales seem dismal, what really matters is the narrative we construct from them. What story will you tell to inspire us?

Note: I paid for my stay at Slebech myself and received no compensation for writing about them.

ENDNOTES

1 Monastic Wales Project (n.d.).' Site details: Slebech'. monasticwales.org. https://monasticwales.org/site/63

2 St Davids Cathedral (n.d.) 'Pilgrimage'. https://www.stdavidscathedral.org.uk/education/pilgrimage

3 Angold, M. J., Gaugh, G. C., Chibnall, M. M., Cox, D. C., Price, D. T. W., Tomlinson, M., & Trinder, B. S. (1973), 'House of Knights Hospitallers: Preceptory of Halston' in Gaydon, A. T. & Pugh, R. B. (eds.) *A History of the Country of Shropshire: Volume 2. British History Online.* https://www.british-history.ac.uk/vch/salop/vol2/pp87-88

4 Guest, C. (tr.) (1877). *The Mabinogion.* London: Bernard Quaritch. p.315.

5 Nicholson, H. J. (2000). *Love, War, and the Grail: Templars, Hospitallers and Teutonic Knights in Medieval Epic and Romance, 1150–1500.* Brill. p.65.

6 Duits, S. (2021). 'The Siege of Smyrna: That Time The Hospitallers Met Timur'. *Medieval Reporter.* https://medievalreporter.com/siege-of-smyrna/

WALES AND STATE SUCCESSION

What happens when a state ceases to exist? A recent article[1] on the Crown Estate in Wales leads me to ponder the question.

As believers in Welsh independence, we seek the breakup of the United Kingdom into three new sovereign states: England, Scotland and Cymru. Northern Ireland will, we assume, reunite with the Republic of Ireland.

This may seem obvious, but we need to start from the basics in order to discuss the question: what becomes of the assets and liabilities of the former UK?

This is going to be of critical importance to us as we embark on the journey towards our future, free of London's rule for the first time in centuries.

Let's talk money.

As of September 2023 (the latest figure available as I write this), the UK's national debt is two trillion, six hundred and fifty-four billion, two hundred million pounds.[2] That's £2,654,200,000,000. The latest available data projected that in the financial year 2021–22 there would be 31.6 million taxpayers in the whole of the UK.[3] In the same tax year, Wales had 1,460,000 taxpayers: 4.62% of the UK total.[4] Using that percentage would give us a share of the UK's national debt equal to £122,624,040,000, or £83,989 per taxpayer in Wales.

I've chosen to count by taxpayer just to illustrate that there are different ways of approaching this. It might be done by the number of people living in Wales, or by only the number of adults. We might count everybody, or only those who had UK citizenship at the time of dissolution. We might count only those who chose Welsh citizenship, regardless of where they are living, and not those (primarily English) who live in Wales but aren't citizens or Green Card holders. There are lots of different ways to address this, and deciding which one we use would be an early and important part of the independence negotiation.

Or we might just say that we will inherit not a single penny of debt and will start with a blank slate.

I need to make it clear at this point that I'm not a lawyer and, particularly, not a specialist in international law. Nevertheless, international law does cover this situation and, like common law in England and Wales, is strongly grounded in precedent. So, what precedents are there in recent times for when a country like the United Kingdom ceases to exist, breaking up into several smaller countries?

As far as I can see, there are two: Yugoslavia and the Soviet Union.

In the first case, Yugoslavia completely disappeared and was replaced by Croatia, Serbia, Slovenia, Bosnia and Herzegovina, and the Republic of Macedonia. (Kosovo separated from Serbia, but later.) Yugoslavia's assets and liabilities were divided between these states.

Each of them joined the United Nations as new states, while Yugoslavia's seat disappeared.

In the second case, the Russian Federation asserted itself as the successor state of the USSR, and was recognised as such by the international community. Russia thereby inherited the Soviet seat on the United Nations Security Council, the USSR's reserves and other international assets, and continued to be bound by the treaties signed by the Soviets. However, it also took on the whole of the Soviet Union's national debt, paying it off completely by 2017. The other former Soviet republics became independent countries with the assets that were within their borders, and with no inherited debt.

Now, it's very common for Unionists to try to frighten the Welsh people with dark warnings about the dire consequences of inherited debt for the Welsh economy after independence. In fact, the only country that will face problems is England, regardless of the precedent that's followed, be it Yugoslav or Soviet – and which one it will be will depend on England alone.

That's because, being far and away the largest and most populous of the four nations, it will be up to England to decide whether or not it follows Russia's example.

If it doesn't, then the UK's national debt will be shared between the newly independent countries. It wouldn't be up to London to dictate the allocation, though.

First of all, they would need to persuade the Irish government that it should accept Northern Ireland's share of UK debt, which wouldn't be certain. Second, following the Yugoslav precedent, debtors' representatives and international bodies such as the IMF would participate in the negotiations, as well as the new states. Third, the Yugoslav precedent would distribute the debt proportionally, according to the benefit received.[5] It would NOT be on a per capita or other population basis.

Given that Wales has historically experienced chronic underinvestment, England would almost certainly have to take on the bulk of the debt; the Welsh share would be very small. Sorry, Unionist fear-mongers.

Furthermore, in this scenario, England, like Wales and Scotland, would become just another ordinary member of the UN General Assembly.[6] The UK's seat at the Security Council would be reallocated to a country with a better claim, such as India.

Given the attitudes that we see dominating Westminster, I find it difficult to imagine England accepting this dramatic fall in international stature. It's more likely that it would follow Russia's example, becoming the legal successor state of the United Kingdom. If it did, it would retain the UK's position in international affairs, including the Security Council seat and all existing treaties. It would also, however, have to assume the entirety of the UK's national debt, which might make its financial status very dubious.

That, of course, would be their problem, not ours.

So, to return to Gwern Gwynfil's article on the Crown Estate: the Estate is not devolved in Wales as it is in Scotland. However, ever since the reign of George III, the revenues of the Crown Estate have been managed by the government – meaning, the accounts are available and we will be able to determine a figure for all the wealth extracted from Wales by the Crown since 1760 up until independence. To this, we will be able to add the billions taken from us for HS2, and all of the other instances in which Wales has been short-changed. No doubt our accountants will be able to work out the interest due as well. We'll be asking for it all back during the independence negotiations – either to further reduce our debt, in a Yugoslav scenario, or as a claim against the UK assets that England would inherit in a Russian scenario. It's not lost to us for ever; it's just a loan under duress to England, and we will see it repaid.

The independence movements in the Celtic countries also need to start lawyering up and putting international lenders on notice that the dissolution of the UK will affect them – discovering who will be affected, identifying who might need to be involved in the negotiations, and beginning the process of building friendly relationships with them.

It's time to stop talking about independence in general terms. It's time to start making detailed preparations. It's time to know what international law says, who the players will be and how we're going to work with them. Let's get ready to make our case.

ENDNOTES

1   Mansfield, M. (2024). 'State sponsored theft?' nation. cymru. https://nation.cymru/opinion/state-sponsored-theft/

2   Office for National Statistics (2024). 'UK government debt and deficit.' www.ons.gov.uk. https://www.ons.gov.uk/economy/governmentpublicsectorandtaxes/publicspending/bulletins/ukgovernmentdebtanddeficitforeurostatmaast/september2023

3   HM Revenue and Customs (n.d.). 'Summary Statistics'. *GOV.UK.* https://www.gov.uk/government/statistics/income-tax-liabilities-statistics-tax-year-2018-to-2019-to-tax-year-2021-to-2022/summary-statistics

4   HM Revenue & Customs (2023). 'Table 2.2 Number of Income Tax payers by country'. *GOV.UK.* https://www.gov.uk/government/statistics/number-of-individual-income-taxpayers-by-marginal-rate-gender-and-age-by-country

5   Stahn, C. (2002). 'The Agreement on Succession Issues of the Former Socialist Federal Republic of Yugoslavia'. *American Journal of International Law*, 96(2). pp.379–397. https://doi.org/10.2307/2693933

6   United Nations Association (2017). 'What would happen to the UK's seat at the UN Security Council if Scotland were to become independent?' 30 Aug. https://una.org.uk/news/what-would-happen-uk%E2%80%99s-seat-un-security-council-if-scotland-were-become-independent

DECOLONISING THE WELSH MIND

'Y Gwir Yn Erbyn Y Byd.' (The Truth Against the World)

'The Anglo-Saxon media will tell outright lies.'

The first of these quotes will be familiar to most Welsh-speakers: it comes from Iolo Morganwg, the eighteenth-century poet, stonemason and radical, who made it a central theme of his legacy. As for the second, I'll tell you below who said it, but taken together, these quotes represent a challenge for Wales as it builds up its separate identity: the decolonisation of our minds.

Iolo walked the talk. As an anti-monarchist, anti-slavery campaigner and Unitarian opponent of the Church of England, not to mention a supporter of the American and French revolutions (Tom Paine was a friend; George Washington subscribed to his books of poetry), Iolo was under constant suspicion of sedition. He was interrogated by cabinet ministers about his politics; magistrates backed up by cavalry broke up Gorsedd meetings, spies shadowed him. And yet, to the end of his life, he continued to fight for his principles despite his own desperate poverty, treating the sick with traditional herbal medicine and giving free legal assistance to those in need.

Despite this, many people immediately roll their eyes at the mention of Iolo Morganwg, dismissing him as an opium addict or a literary forger, and refusing to consider him further. Why is that?

They do it because they have a story in their head, one that tells them how to think and feel in response to Iolo's name. We all do it, all the time, in all kinds of circumstances. It's an evolutionary response, hardwired into our brains: it's the only way we can function without totally overburdening our cognitive abilities. The 'stories' trigger an automatic response, allowing us to reserve mental capacity for novel situations, which demand more processing.

We primarily acquire these stories as children, from our families and local community –versions of the stories of the broader culture we live in. As we get older, we ourselves modify the stories we were given and acquire new ones, as a result of our unique, personal experiences.

Problems arise when the stories are wrong, incomplete or obsolete. In that case, our responses, and our subsequent decisions and actions, are going to be inappropriate. That can happen because a story isn't accurately communicated, or when times have changed but the story hasn't. What's more, stories can be deliberately shaped to ensure that we think in ways that benefit people other than ourselves.

Why do so many people, often those who should know better, have this fixed image of Iolo Morganwg as a drug-addicted faker? It often seems that they will condemn Iolo's use of laudanum even while celebrating his friend Coleridge – and many others – for doing the same.

I really can't say for sure why they do this. I will note, though, that if people understood who Iolo really was and what he did, he would be a powerful icon for those who believe that Wales should cultivate a strong and resilient Welsh-speaking civilisation, and for those who believe Wales should be independent. Deliberately propagating a narrative that leads people to instantly dismiss him clearly benefits those who are threatened by one or both of these causes.

Unfortunately, most people don't know the facts about Iolo or, really, about anything outside their personal experience. That's why, when people watch the news, they may well be very annoyed by inaccuracies on a topic they know about, but they'll still accept everything else as accurate and true. This is a recognised phenomenon known as the Gell-Mann Amnesia effect[1] or Knoll's Law of Media Accuracy.[2] It allows those who control the media to control the messages it conveys – and the stories that will henceforth be embedded in our minds, determining our future responses. When people in Wales are being conditioned to think in ways that benefit elites outside Wales, rather than in ways that serve our own interests and cultural values, then their minds are being colonised. I think here of the people who tried to make a controversy out of the Llangollen Eisteddfod's motto, based on linguistic associations derived from English that don't apply to Welsh.[3] I don't know anybody involved, but my impression is of colonised minds, speaking Welsh yet Anglo-Saxon in their thinking.

So, who said 'The Anglo-Saxon media will tell outright lies'? It was veteran Singaporean diplomat and academic, Kishore Mahbubani.[4] Mahbubani – who is globally respected and highly influential – was giving a brief talk on the South China Sea. Many readers will have seen the London media describing China's aggressive and expansionary policies in the region. This, explained Mahbubani, is factually untrue; indeed, it's the opposite of the truth. I'd urge you to take a few minutes to watch the video, if you can.[5]

A former director of MI6 warns that none of the UK's foreign intelligence services have any real understanding of China's motivations and reasoning.[6] Instead, it would seem, they apply stories from other contexts and then act as if this represents reality. The media take their lead from what the government says, and the population ends up believing things that are completely inaccurate – and this is just as true about other countries currently in the headlines.

Using Critical Discourse Analysis to evaluate reporting across different media outlets in this way (particularly if it's the same across the political spectrum) would alert the careful reader that something is amiss. Unfortunately, most readers have never heard of it, let alone make a habit of it.

This threat was recognised in the 1980s by Derrick Hearne who, in *The Joy of Freedom*,[7] discussed 'Programmed Social Response'.[8] It's something that those whose loyalty is to Wales must learn to recognise, so we can use Critical Discourse Analysis to identify any attempts to manipulate our thinking. There are resources online for this; one that I can recommend from personal experience is The Stories We Live By, a free short course offered by the University of Gloucester.[9]

For practice, read this 2017 article from The Guardian about Welsh-medium education in Llangennech, in Carmarthenshire: '"We're told we're anti-Welsh bigots and fascists" – the storm over Welsh-first schooling'.[10] Consider who is named and who is left un-named. What kind of adjectives are used about the different sides? Is one side more relatable than the other? Is emotive language used? If so, why? Statistics are given, but are they convincing? Is full context given, or are relevant facts omitted?[11]

Here in Wales, we must remember that, although the British Empire is history, London remains colonial in its thinking, and the media continue to serve its imperial purposes. We know that the UK media doesn't represent us fully nor accurately, and that we need more local sources. We're going to learn that much of what we think we know about the world isn't true; that it's been misrepresented to suit someone's agenda. As another example, did you know that, notwithstanding the presence of antisemitism there as elsewhere, Viktor Orbán's 'far right' Hungary is one of the safest countries in Europe for Jews – to the extent that Jews from elsewhere in Europe are relocating there? You probably didn't if you get your worldview from the UK media. And yet it's a fact openly discussed in Jewish media.[12] Why isn't this more widely reported, do you think?

So, let's emulate Iolo Morganwg. Seek the truth and defend it. Learn to identify the methods the media use to manipulate your thinking. Check the validity of your beliefs. Decolonise your mind. Be free!

ENDNOTES

[1] The Basics Guide. (2023). 'Gell-Mann Amnesia Effect'. https://thebasics.guide/gell-mann-amnesia-effect/

[2] Shatz, I. (n.d.). 'Knoll's Law of Media Accuracy: Remember that Not Everything in the News Is True'. *Effectiviology*. https://effectiviology.com/knolls-law/

[3] Anon. (2023). 'Llangollen Eisteddfod decides to keep motto despite racism fears'. *BBC News*. 11 Apr. https://www.bbc.co.uk/news/uk-wales-65238624

[4] Mahbubani, K. (n.d.). 'About Kishore Mahbubani'. *Kishore Mahbubani*. https://mahbubani.net/about/

[5] Mothership Singapore (2024). 'Sessions With: History of Trade Routes (featuring Kishore Mahbubani)'. *www.youtube.com*. https://youtu.be/kg8TmKuaYAQ?si=1ZvUUb4txtZ6xhnQ

[6] Anon. (2024). 'Ex-MI6 boss warns UK not equipped to deal with Chinese spies'. ITV News. 27 Jan. https://www.itv.com/news/2024-01-27/ex-mi6-boss-voices-fears-over-british-intelligence-blind-spot-with-beijing

[7] Hearne, D. (1977). *The Joy of Freedom*. Talybont: Y Lolfa.

8   Pasterski, M. (2020). 'Social programming' . *Pasterski*. https://pasterski.com/2020/08/social-programming/

9   Stibbe, A. (n.d.). 'Ecolinguistics: The Stories We Live By'. *University of Gloucester*. https://www.storiesweliveby.org.uk

10   Tickle, L. and Morris, S. (2017). '"We're told we're anti-Welsh bigots and fascists" – the storm over Welsh-first schooling'. *The Guardian*. https://www.theguardian.com/education/2017/jun/20/storm-welsh-only-schools-minority-language

11   Llangennech was the home of pioneering Welsh-language campaigners Eileen and Trefor Beasley.

     See: Stephens, M. (2012). 'The Rosa Parks of the Welsh language movement'. *Institute of Welsh Affairs*. https://www.iwa.wales/agenda/2012/10/the-rosa-parks-of-the-welsh-language-movement/

12   (i) Veszprémy, L. B. (2022). 'As Europe Sees Rise in Antisemitism, Hungary Remains Safe Haven for Jews'. *Newsweek*. https://www.newsweek.com/europe-sees-rise-antisemitism-hungary-remains-safe-haven-jews-opinion-1728027

     ii) Israel, D. (2022). 'Study: Least Friendly Countries to Jews in Europe: Belgium & Poland; Friendliest: Italy & Hungary'. *The Jewish Press*. https://www.jewishpress.com/news/jewish-news/study-least-friendly-countries-to-jews-in-europe-belgium-friendliest-italy-hungary/2022/06/21/

(iii) Ben-Nunn, S. (2022). 'Which European countries are keeping Jews the safest?' *The Jerusalem Post.* https://www.jpost.com/diaspora/article-709915

(iv) Liphshiz, C. (2022). 'Which European countries are best for Jews? A new study offers unexpected answers'. *Jewish Telegraphic Agency.* https://www.jta.org/2022/06/21/global/which-european-countries-are-best-for-jews-a-new-study-offers-unexpected-answers

WALES AND SINGAPORE

As the discussion over Welsh independence heats up, it's time to start looking beyond it and consider how the country should be governed and made a success.

Some might wish there were a manual on how to lead a new country. Well, the good news is that one does actually exist. The bad news is that it makes clear the extent of the difficulties that we will face – and they are substantial. Studying it will at least show aspiring national leaders what they will have to do.

First, though, let's establish some context. The growing conversation[1] about what independence might look like for Wales is an urgent one: the UK appears to be becoming a failed state.[2]

It's popular to argue that we have a population comparable in size to many of the smaller EU members. The Baltic states, or former Yugoslav republics such as Slovenia are often evoked as evidence that an independent Wales could succeed. Some caution is needed here, though. Both the Soviet Union and Yugoslavia were federal states. When they broke up and their constituent republics became independent, their politicians and bureaucracies already had many decades' worth of experience in autonomous policy development and decision-making. Wales will lack this depth of experience when it leaves the UK.

The former Soviet and Yugoslav republics also became independent at a fortuitous time. They were welcomed with open arms by the EU, with which free trade agreements were soon signed. Becoming members was a smooth process. Their independence came at a time of cheap and abundant energy, when investment was plentiful and when global markets were opening up. To the east, Russia was focused on its own problems, and anyway aspired to integrate economically with the EU, 'from Lisbon to Vladivostok'. Independence was thus relatively pain-free, both diplomatically and economically.

Wales will not be so fortunate. England – sullen and diminished – is likely to be a troublesome and obstructive neighbour. The EU, which once promised subsidiarity, is becoming more top-down, demanding a move to majority votes for both internal and external policy and – horrifyingly – actually prepared plans to deliberately crash the economy of a member state,[3] which would plunge millions of EU citizens into poverty to punish a government for resisting centralisation. That's unacceptable.

Meanwhile, globalisation is unwinding, the costs of energy and raw materials are growing and instability is spreading. We need to be realistic: independent Wales will effectively be a developing country. It may very well be that joining the BRICS group would offer better opportunities.[4]

Supporters of Welsh independence must therefore look further afield to find an example to emulate: 6,872 miles further as the Airbus flies, to be specific.

Singapore gained its independence in a chaotic manner when it was expelled from Malaysia in 1965. Its leaders were inexperienced. The British had only established the Legislative Assembly a decade before; Lee Kwan Yew and his People's Action Party had only formed a government in 1959. Its largest and closest neighbours, Malaysia and Indonesia, were in armed confrontation with each other, and neither was well-disposed towards Singapore. The new nation had no natural resources and little industry. Much of its population lived in slums, and it was riven by tensions between ethnic groups that, under British rule, had largely lived largely separate lives.

Remarkably, Lee and his fellow ministers overcame these very substantial obstacles and transformed their city-state into a globally admired success. Dr Edward Jones, an economist at Bangor University, recently wrote a valuable article about this: 'For Wales, see Singapore? A strategy for independence'.[5] It is, though, very much an economist's article and reminds me of a joke about that profession: 'Assume a can-opener...'[6] It makes many assumptions, disguising the reality that Singapore's success was actually very hard-won indeed, and was very far from guaranteed. Wales may struggle to emulate it.

Lee Kwan Yew – an outstandingly talented man and a great statesman – recorded the process in his memoirs, *From Third World to First.*[7] This is, in effect, a manual for governing a new nation. It should be read, reread and read again by everyone who aspires to creating a prosperous, sovereign Wales.

The question we must ask is: if we want to achieve the prosperity that Lee brought to Singapore, are we willing to use his methods?

Many will balk at this. Lee decided on a clear goal: to make Singapore clean and green compared to neighbouring countries, a First World haven in a Third World region. To make this a reality, the city and its people would have to be transformed to conform with Lee's vision, willingly or not.

The people were to speak the languages decreed by the state; if they couldn't or wouldn't, their children would be educated in those languages anyway. Citizens were expected to behave in a cultivated and community-minded manner. If they chose not to, well, they would be made to.

Drugs undermine social values, so drug-trafficking warrants a mandatory death sentence, even for 1 kg of cannabis.[8] Using drugs and other offences warrant physical punishment by caning,[9] leaving lasting physical and psychological scars.[10] Plain-clothes police are ever-watchful for crimes such as littering.[11] These and other anti-social behaviours such as spitting are heavily fined.

To keep his new society honest, Lee instituted merciless anti-corruption laws[12] and saw that government ministers were paid millions, equivalent to multi-national CEOs.[13] His Singapore became a strict meritocracy: academic high-achievers were identified and cultivated for promotion through the ranks. Political opposition faced tough libel laws,[14] with critics receiving massive fines,[15] often bankrupted or even forced into exile.[16]

Substandard housing was summarily demolished and replaced with publicly owned apartments. Tax incentives encourage families both to improve their level of education and to have three or four children. Looking after elderly relatives is required by law.[17]

Singapore's admirers also often skim over the uncomfortable fact that much of its success rests on the hundreds of thousands of migrant workers from India and Bangladesh, who live crammed into barracks, isolated from the bulk of the population.[18] Not to mention the tens of thousands of low-paid maids from Indonesia and the Philippines, who free up Singapore's middle class for office jobs.[19]

I don't write this to criticise Singapore. Lee's government had to work with what they had, and they succeeded. It helped that Asian cultures are more collectivist and respectful of authority than European cultures, so the population was largely supportive.[20] The world now looks at the results with envy.

Nevertheless, a newly independent Wales will face many of the same domestic and international challenges that confronted Singapore. Like them, our legacy from London's rule will be widespread social deprivation, poverty and rejection of education.[21] We have suffered from massive underinvestment in people, property and infrastructure. We will need to decide on a clear national vision and will have to make it happen.

Could the Welsh accept Singaporean discipline? Could we prioritise collective well-being over individual freedoms, as Singaporeans have? If we aren't willing to be as single-minded and ruthless as Lee Kwan Yew, well, we will need to discover other, equally effective ways to create the future Wales. It won't be easy. But we need to be ready for the challenges we will face.

ENDNOTES

1   Hobson, S. (2024). 'A future of our design: mapping an independent Cymru'. *Bylines Cymru*. https://bylines. cymru/voices-lleisiau/independent-cymru-map/

2   (i) Mansfield, M. (2024). 'The report of the Welsh Government's Constitutional Commission is both a challenge and an opportunity for the Welsh Lib Dems'. *Nation.Cymru*. https://nation.cymru/opinion/ the-report-of-the-welsh-governments-constitutional-commission-is-both-a-challenge-and-an-opportunity-for-the-welsh-lib-dems/

(ii) Watkins, T. (2024). 'Broken'. *The Consciousness of Sheep*. https://consciousnessofsheep.co.uk/2024/02/22/ broken/

3   O'Carroll, L. (2024). 'Secret EU plan "to sabotage Hungarian economy" revealed as anger mounts at Orbán'. *The Guardian*. 29 Jan. https://www. theguardian.com/world/2024/jan/29/secret-eu-plan-to-sabotage-hungarian-economy-revealed-as-anger-mounts-at-orban

4   CGTN (2023). 'Explainer: Why do more countries want to join BRICS?' *CGTN Africa*. https://africa.

cgtn.com/explainer-why-do-more-countries-want-to-join-brics/

[5] Jones, E. T. (2024). 'For Wales, see Singapore? A strategy for independence'. *Institute of Welsh Affairs*. https://www.iwa.wales/agenda/2024/01/constitutional-commission-welsh-independence/

[6] As Wikipedia says, this 'is a catchphrase used to mock economists and other theorists who base their conclusions on unjustified or oversimplified assumptions'.

Anon (2023). 'Assume a can opener'. *Wikipedia*. https://en.wikipedia.org/wiki/Assume_a_can_opener

[7] Lee, K. Y. (2000). *From Third World to First. The Singapore Story: 1965–2000*. New York: Harper.

[8] Hancock, A. (2023). 'Singapore's death row "main element of its drug policy"'. *www.aljazeera.com*. https://www.aljazeera.com/news/2023/5/16/singapores-death-row-main-element-of-its-drug-policy

[9] JCP Law LLC (2024). 'Caning in Singapore – What Does the Law Say.' *Legal Advice Singapore*. https://legaladvice.com.sg/caning-in-singapore

[10] Lay, B. (2022). 'Changi Prison inmate describes getting 21 strokes of cane in 10 mins: "From 1 to 10 is very pain already"'. *mothership.sg*. https://mothership.sg/2022/09/caning-jail-singapore-experience/

[11] Tan, A. (2014). 'Plain clothes officers target litterbugs in latest NEA enforcement blitz'. *The Straits Times*. 12

Apr. https://www.straitstimes.com/singapore/courts-crime/plain-clothes-officers-target-litterbugs-in-latest-nea-enforcement-blitz

[12] Corrupt Practices Investigation Bureau (n.d.). 'Prevention Of Corruption Act'. *www.cpib.gov.sg*. https://www.cpib.gov.sg/about-corruption/legislation-and-enforcement/prevention-of-corruption-act/

[13] Tham, D. (2023). 'CNA Explains: How are political salaries in Singapore calculated?' *Channel News Asia*. https://www.channelnewsasia.com/singapore/minister-salary-review-political-appointment-holder-3198201

[14] Evans, T. (2015). 'Lee Kuan Yew and freedom of expression: the libel action as a means of silencing political opposition'. *Inforrm's Blog*. 26 Mar. https://inforrm.org/2015/03/26/lee-kuan-yew-and-freedom-of-expression-the-libel-action-as-a-means-of-silencing-political-opposition-tessa-evans/

[15] Reuters (2021). 'Singapore blogger ordered to pay nearly US$100,000 damages to PM for Facebook post'. *The Guardian*. 25 Mar. https://www.theguardian.com/world/2021/mar/25/singapore-blogger-ordered-to-pay-nearly-us100000-damages-to-pm-for-facebook-post

[16] Jeyaretnam, K. (2012). 'Disneyland With the Death Penalty, Revisited'. *Wired*. 10 Apr. https://www.wired.com/2012/04/opinion-jeyaretnam-disneyland-death-penalty/

17   Hartung, R. (2019). 'Children taking care of parents' needs: Changing norms and what to expect'. *TODAYonline*. https://www.todayonline.com/singapore/ children-taking-care-parents-needs-changing-norms- and-what-expect

18   Tan, Y. (2020). 'Covid-19 Singapore: A "pandemic of inequality" exposed'. BBC News. 18 Sep. https://www. bbc.co.uk/news/world-asia-54082861

19   L. H. (n.d.). 'Domestic Helpers in Singapore: What to Do When They Arrive'. *Homage*. https://www.homage. sg/resources/new-maid-what-to-do/

20   The Culture Factor Group (n.d.). 'Country comparison tool'. *www.hofstede-insights.com*. https://www.hofstede- insights.com/country-comparison-tool?countries=china %2Cindia%2Cmalaysia%2Cunited+kingdom

21   Lewis, A. (2024).' The shocking figures of school absenteeism in a Welsh town'. *Nation.Cymru*. https:// nation.cymru/news/the-shocking-figures-of-school- absenteeism-in-a-welsh-town/

WELSH DRAGONS IN THE SEA

The Dragon in the Sea is an early novel by Frank Herbert, who later become famous for *Dune* and its sequels. His story is a psychological drama about submariners under intense mental stress. It's of particular interest because, in the story, the submarines are transporting oil contained in enormous plastic bags towed behind the vessel and floating just below the surface of the ocean.

Herbert researched his themes in great depth. His idea was scientifically valid, having been developed in the 1950s at Cambridge University, and was later turned into a commercially viable reality by private companies, becoming known – in tribute to the novel – as Dracone barges. Today, they are widely used around the world to transport many kinds of liquids, including water.

So, what's this got to do with Wales? The answer is: climate change.

If you live in Wales, or have visited, you've probably noticed that it rains here. Quite a lot. As the oceans warm up, they will release more moisture into the atmosphere, which will turn into more rain; it's predicted that the UK in particular is going have even wetter weather than it does now.[1] What's not going to change is Britain's physical geography; those clouds will still pile in from the Atlantic, be forced upwards over the Welsh mountains and shed their contents onto Wales. So, we're going to get lots more rain, much more than we currently do. People living next to the 327 high-risk coal tips in the Valleys already worry whenever it rains[2] – the risk of another Aberfan-style disaster is only going to increase.

Meanwhile, the same climatic changes are making the Mediterranean region hotter and drier.[3] Spain, for example, is facing extended and worsening droughts, with many communities facing restrictions on water use, or even needing to have their water brought in from elsewhere as local sources run out.[4] Increasingly, the authorities are being forced to rely on desalinated sea water – an energy-intensive and expensive process. This same pattern is being seen all around the Mediterranean.

Could Welsh water be a part of their response? Let's look at some numbers.

Cape Town, with a Mediterranean climate on the southern tip of Africa, demonstrates the problems that are coming. In 2017–18, a prolonged drought brought the city to breaking point; despite ultra-strict restrictions on water use, the city came close to running out entirely – a prospect identified as 'Day Zero'.[5] The rains returned at the last minute and the crisis was averted, but not before discussions were held about shipping in water in fleets of supertankers, or even towing icebergs to the gasping population.[6] Desalinisation doesn't seem to have been discussed; it was likely too expensive for a developing nation.

Cape Town has a population of four million people and needs 500 million litres of fresh water every day. One supertanker can transport 400 million litres, but that's only the largest ships; most carry less than that. So, a city like Cape Town would need a minimum of two ships delivering fresh water every single day, and perhaps more.

Dracone barges, by way of comparison, can carry up to 1.1 million litres in the largest sizes: nothing like a supertanker's capacity.[7] However, they can be towed for hundreds of miles in the open sea by a relatively small and inexpensive tug. A fleet of tugs equipped with Dracone barges might be cheaper and more versatile than a fleet of supertankers.[8]

How much fresh water could Wales export? According to the BBC and the Senedd, Dŵr Cymru sells 320 million litres to Severn Trent Water every day for use in England,[9] and United Utilities takes 302 million every day. That gives a total of roughly 622 million litres of water currently exported from Wales every single day. However, England plans to extract a further 155 million litres daily,[10] so we're looking at a potential daily capacity of 777 million litres: half as much again as needed for a city like Cape Town. Barcelona, in drought-stricken Catalonia, with its surrounding region, has 4.6 million people, making the two cities roughly comparable. Welsh water shipped to Barcelona would likely be cheaper than desalinated water – and would allow the increasingly expensive energy to be used for other purposes.

Wales alone can't solve Spain's water problem, but it could make a significant contribution while that country adapts to climate change. It could, likewise, make a difference in Italy, Greece or Morocco. As we receive more rain in the future, so will we be able to export more – assuming we invest in improving the size and number of our reservoirs.

But isn't that water already accounted for? It goes to England, after all...

An independent Wales would nationalise our water reserves and cancel those contracts. Thereafter, our surplus water might be sold at international auction, perhaps (to use a figure chosen completely at random) in tranches of 10 million litres/day for a period of five years. England could still buy our water, of course, but they would have to beat the offers coming in from other countries.

Water sold to overseas buyers could be shipped in a fleet of supertankers, which would probably mean developing our main deep-water harbour at Milford Haven as the export hub. Alternatively, flotillas of much smaller tugs towing Dracone barges might create a network of smaller hubs around the Welsh coast, with the added benefit of revitalising our ancient maritime communities and small ports, and kickstarting a Welsh merchant navy. It wasn't that long ago, after all, that Wales had a fleet of small ships criss-crossing its waters, and tramp steamers, officered and crewed entirely by Welsh-speakers, that were frequent visitors to ports and harbours around the world. Imagine fleets of Welsh 'dragon barges', crewed and captained by Cymry Cymraeg, sailing the high seas...

Raising the investment to establish this fleet and the necessary infrastructure should be straightforward; the business model speaks for itself and is sustainable for the long term. The key point is that selling our water on an international market is feasible. We're not locked in to selling to England.

What about the communities in England who currently receive Welsh water? Of course, they can still have it – if they pay us the best price. In any case, England may well be getting wetter as well. However, the Environment Agency recently predicted that, by 2025, England will need an extra five billion litres per day, over and above the current daily usage of fourteen billion.[11] Five billion! They are going to have much bigger water problems than they can solve with what they get from Wales. Perhaps they can invest in building reservoirs in their own country. It's not for us to worry about, though. Charity begins at home, and London's rule has left Wales with many expensive problems to be addressed – such as those coal tips.

Nevertheless, the threat of losing cheap water is one reason why London will fight tooth and nail to prevent Welsh independence. This should motivate us to struggle even harder to achieve it: to establish control over our natural resources and finally receive fair value for them, for the benefit of our own people. Here's one way we can do it.

ENDNOTES

1   Met Office (2022). 'Climate change in the UK'. *Met Office*. https://www.metoffice.gov.uk/weather/climate-change/climate-change-in-the-uk

2   Fyfe, W. (2022). 'Climate change: Living by coal tip leaves family fearing rain'. *BBC News*. 1 Jan. https://www.bbc.co.uk/news/uk-wales-59653955

3   IPCC (n.d.). 'Cross-Chapter Paper 4: Mediterranean Region'. *www.ipcc.ch*. https://www.ipcc.ch/report/ar6/wg2/chapter/ccp4/

4   Euronews Green and AP (2024). 'Drought-stricken villages in Spain are bringing in water in tankers'. *euronews*. https://www.euronews.com/green/2024/02/02/a-new-climate-reality-spains-drought-stricken-villages-have-been-in-crisis-mode-for-months

5   Edmond, C. (2019). 'Cape Town almost ran out of water. Here's how it averted the crisis'. *World Economic Forum*. https://www.weforum.org/agenda/2019/08/cape-town-was-90-days-away-from-running-out-of-water-heres-how-it-averted-the-crisis/

6   Valentine, H. (2020). 'Transporting Potable Water by Sea'. *The Maritime Executive*. https://maritime-

executive.com/editorials/transporting-potable-water-by-sea

7   SHERWOOD Media s.r.o (n.d.). 'Dracone Barge'. *Rubena.eu*. https://www.rubena.eu/en/products/flexible-and-inflatable-rubber-products/dracone-barge

8   trends.directindustry.com. (n.d.). 'The Dracone Barge a truly flexible bulk liquid transport solution by Dunlop'. *DirectIndustry*. https://trends.directindustry.com/dunlop-grg/project-121457-135469.html

9   (i) Frampton, B. (2018). 'UK heatwave: How much water does Wales pump to England?' *BBC News*. 28 Jul. https://www.bbc.co.uk/news/uk-wales-44966131

      (ii) Senedd Research (2023). 'Exporting Wales' water: How much and where to?' *research.senedd.wales*. https://research.senedd.wales/research-articles/exporting-wales-water-how-much-and-where-to/

10   Forgrave, A. (2023). 'Huge pipeline plan to take water from Wales to London nears critical decision'. *North Wales Live*. https://www.dailypost.co.uk/news/north-wales-news/huge-pipeline-plan-take-water-26376163

11   Environment Agency (n.d.). 'A summary of England's draft regional and water resources management plans'. *GOV.UK*. https://www.gov.uk/government/publications/a-review-of-englands-draft-regional-and-water-resources-management-plans/a-summary-of-englands-draft-regional-and-water-resources-management-plans

AN ANCIENT EDUCATION FOR A FUTURE WALES

In a recent article,[1] I discussed scenario planning exercises; that is, combining current trends and trying to imagine how the combination will develop, what the consequences might be and what strategies might be needed in response.[2] One such exercise leads me to wonder about our education system. In a free Wales, what do we want it to achieve?

Iolo Morganwg was a stonemason who worked with marble, something only the best could do. He was a poet whose English works influenced both Coleridge and Wordsworth, and whose Welsh poetry equalled that of the best bards of the past. His musical knowledge allowed him to preserve the vanishing folk music and songs of his time.

He was able to design and build buildings – and the furniture to go inside them. He became an expert in agricultural improvement. As an antiquarian, he could analyse and evaluate the mortar in Iron Age forts.

Which trends lead me to think of Iolo's cross-disciplinary virtuosity? Automation and AI.

In Wales, we're still talking about saving jobs in Port Talbot's steelworks; in China, more and more steel mills are fully automated.[3] These days, China is still a low-cost manufacturer, but because their factories are 'lights out', using robots rather than migrant workers from the countryside.[4] This doesn't mean that China's workers aren't important anymore. As Apple CEO Tim Cook explains, China provides not only highly skilled programmers but also world-class tooling engineers and vocational know-how.[5]

Meanwhile, developments in technology bring us huge economic challenges. AI software is producing short videos of astonishing quality, and will soon be able to create entire movies.[6] It can already generate 'talking heads' which are indistinguishable from real people in online communication.[7]

Any job based on knowledge and abstract thinking can increasingly be done by software. The creative industries. Doctors. Accountants. Lawyers. Copywriters. Recruitment. Even schoolteachers and university lecturers. Everything that these professions can do in a Zoom call can be done by AI.[8] The client probably won't even realise they haven't interacted with a human – and the painful truth is that, according to research, AI may often do it better and cheaper.[9] And these are early days.[10]

How do we respond to this? Where should we target our investments? I don't think anybody knows.

It's clear, though, that we need to fundamentally reform our education model, which has long been recognised as out of date, emphasising standardisation at the expense of creativity. It's a real problem in Wales, and it's of particular concern for our national future that

Welsh- medium schools perform worse[11] than English-medium ones.

Interaction between the arts and engineers is essential for technological breakthroughs and innovation. An artistic outlook, looking at things in different sensory ways, combined with mathematical talent, drives our understanding of fundamental science; some of the greatest scientists – Einstein or Feynman, for example – are also creatives and artists.

More than this, we need to be teaching in-demand technical and vocational skills more widely.

Iolo Morganwg could do what he did because of his education, which enabled him to become highly proficient in all subjects in which he later took an interest. He learned his practical skills from his father, a mason and builder. From his gentry-born mother, he received a gentleman's education influenced by the Trivium and the Quadrivium.[12]

The Trivium included Grammar, Logic and Rhetoric. Grammar taught the careful and correct use of language; Logic taught questioning, reasoning and how to identify flawed or misleading arguments; Rhetoric taught the expression of views in a well-structured and persuasive manner.

The Quadrivium, which followed, was Arithmetic, Geometry, Astronomy and Music. Together, these subjects taught an integrated understanding of the importance of numbers. Geometry plays a major part in Islamic art, just as it does in Christian and Buddhist art, and in the design of Hindu temples.[13] Once you understand the Golden

Ratio, the Golden Spiral and Fibonacci Numbers, you can understand everything from how music works, to beauty in architecture, to the shapes of plants and seashells and the movement of the planets.[14] Not to mention, of course, making you a better carpenter.[15]

This system produces adults who have a command of literature, public speaking, analysis and argument. They can go on to specialise in art, music, accounting, programming, design, architecture and anything else grounded in mathematics and logic. Furthermore, the insight that the growth of plants, musical scales and the movement of the planets obey the same mathematical principles illuminates the underlying unity of the universe: a precursor to discussions of religious faith and philosophy.

From the late Roman Empire to the early twentieth century, the Trivium and Quadrivium together formed the seven 'liberal arts'. Craft and trade skills might be needed to make a living, but the liberal arts make a free and independent mind.

This was well understood in the nineteenth-century United States. Educators needed a practical syllabus providing the skills to manage farm finances as well as design and build farmhouses and barns. They were also very conscious that they were a new society, and that if the young American republic was to succeed it needed articulate, rational citizens who could develop and express informed opinions about their country, its governance and its place in the wider world. A surviving exam paper from a Kentucky school, set in 1912, shows the breadth and detail of knowledge then expected at the age of 12–13; the questions cover a very broad range, from arithmetic challenges to grammatical theory, human physiology to the titles and roles of civic officials, to the history of science and international affairs.[16]

We should be humble enough to accept that the educators of previous centuries were actually pretty smart and perceptive, and that their methods and goals are very likely more suited to our independent future than our current model, which was inherited from the Industrial Revolution to produce factory workers.

We once understood that some people thrive on abstract thinking, other people thrive in practical activities and some people will thrive in both. And that we need them all. Wales should return to what used to be normal: that all pupils take classes in crafts such as metalwork, woodwork, sewing and how to grow and cook food. Those whose talents lie in these areas will follow a career in the trades or crafts – which, in independent Wales, will mirror the standards of Germany's 'master craftsman' certification.[17] We should establish colleges similar to the American College of the Building Arts, providing an education that combines the liberal arts with master-level craftsmanship.[18]

The abstract thinkers will go on to develop careers in more conceptual fields. Many will do both, like Matt Crawford who combines work as an academic philosopher with being a self-employed motorcycle mechanic.[19]

Some people will go straight from school to university because they know what they want to study, but this shouldn't be the norm. Many people will benefit from going later, after they've knocked about a bit in the world and come to understand what they really want to do.

The future of education lies in the past: a cross-disciplinary system that allows talent to emerge naturally, in its own time, and which develops the citizens a free nation needs. The seven liberal arts were the foundation of education for centuries for good reason. It's time for Wales to return to what worked for so long – and that provides the skillset we need to adapt to new economic realities.

ENDNOTES

1 Phillips, E. (2024). 'Into the future: resource policies in an independent Wales'. *Bylines Cymru*. https://bylines.cymru/voices-lleisiau/future-wales/

2 Wiles, J. (2022). 'What Functional Leaders Should Know About Scenario Planning'. *Gartner*. https://www.gartner.com/smarterwithgartner/what-functional-leaders-should-know-about-scenario-planning

3 (i) info@dbmsteel.com (2023). 'Artificial intelligence in the steel industry: steel mills embrace big data and robots'. *DBM Metallurgical Intelligence*. https://dbmsteel.com/artificial-intelligence-in-the-steel-industry-steel-mills-embrace-big-data-and-robots

   (ii) Yang, G. (2023). 'Digitalization in China's steel industry'. *news.cgtn.com*. https://news.cgtn.com/news/2023-11-23/Digitalization-in-China-s-steel-industry-1oXXJOox8sw/index.html

   (iii) english.www.gov.cn. (2022). 'Drone's-eye view of modern Chinese automated steel plant'. https://english.www.gov.cn/news/videos/202212/27/content_WS63aa54bcc6d0a757729e4d16.html

4   (i) CGTN (2024). 'China's manufacturing goes intelligent with modern factories'. *news.cgtn.com*. https://news.cgtn.com/news/2024-01-19/China-s-manufacturing-goes-intelligent-with-modern-factories-1quv48okSlw/p.html.

(ii) OEEsystems International. (n.d.). 'Fully Automated Factories: The Future Of Manufacturing?' *OEEsystems*. https://www.oeesystems.com/knowledge/fully-automated-factories-future-manufacturing/

5   Leibowitz, G. (2017). 'Apple CEO Tim Cook: This Is the Number 1 Reason We Make iPhones in China (It's Not What You Think)'. *Inc.com*. https://www.inc.com/glenn-leibowitz/apple-ceo-tim-cook-this-is-number-1-reason-we-make-iphones-in-china-its-not-what-you-think.html

6   (i) McDermott, E. (2023). 'AI Decision-Making in Hollywood Is Already Here, Now What?' *The Hollywood Reporter*. https://www.hollywoodreporter.com/business/digital/ai-filmmaking-algorithm-documentaries-non-fiction-1235478174/

(ii) Wilson, M. (2024). '11 mind-blowing OpenAI Sora videos that show it's another ChatGPT moment for AI'. *TechRadar*. https://www.techradar.com/computing/artificial-intelligence/11-mind-blowing-sora-shorts-that-show-why-its-a-chatgpt-moment-for-ai-video

7   (i) Edwards, B. (2024). Microsoft's VASA-1 can deepfake a person with one photo and one audio track. *Ars Technica*. https://arstechnica.com/information-

technology/2024/04/microsofts-vasa-1-can-deepfake-a-person-with-one-photo-and-one-audio-track/

(ii) Xu, S., Chen, G., Guo, Y.-X., Yang, J., Li, C., Zang, Z., Zhang, Y., Tong, X. and Guo, B. (n.d.). 'VASA-1'. *Microsoft Research*. https://www.microsoft.com/en-us/research/project/vasa-1/

8   (i) Cremer, D. D., Bianzino, N. M. and Falk, B. (2023). 'How Generative AI Could Disrupt Creative Work' *Harvard Business Review*. https://hbr.org/2023/04/how-generative-ai-could-disrupt-creative-work

(ii) Leibowitz, D. (2020). '"Sherlock Holmes" AI Diagnoses Disease Better Than Your Doctor, Study Finds'. *Medium*. https://towardsdatascience.com/ai-diagnoses-disease-better-than-your-doctor-study-finds-a5cc0ffbf32

(iii) Finance Voices. (2018). 'Is Artificial Intelligence Set to Replace Accountants in the Future?' *Spiceworks*. https://www.spiceworks.com/tech/artificial-intelligence/articles/is-artificial-intelligence-set-to-replace-accountants-in-the-future/

(iv) Brochner, N. M. (2023). 'Council Post: Will AI Replace Lawyers?' *Forbes*. https://www.forbes.com/sites/forbestechcouncil/2023/05/25/will-ai-replace-lawyers

(v) Williams, H. (2023). 'I'm a copywriter. I'm pretty sure artificial intelligence is going to take my job'. *The Guardian*. https://www.theguardian.com/commentisfree/2023/jan/24/chatgpt-artificial-intelligence-jobs-economy

(vi) Will, P., Krpan, D. and Lordan, G. (2022). 'Artificial Intelligence job hiring outperforms human hiring'. *London School of Economics and Political Science.* https://www.lse.ac.uk/News/Latest-news-from-LSE/2022/e-May-22/Artificial-Intelligence-job-hiring-outperforms-human-hiring

(vii) Devlin, H. (2023). 'AI likely to spell end of traditional school classroom, leading expert says'. *The Guardian.* 7 Jul. https://www.theguardian.com/technology/2023/jul/07/ai-likely-to-spell-end-of-traditional-school-classroom-leading-expert-says

(viii) Haw, M. (2019). 'Will AI replace university lecturers? Not if we make it clear why humans matter'. *The Guardian.* 6 Sep. https://www.theguardian.com/education/2019/sep/06/will-ai-replace-university-lecturers-not-if-we-make-it-clear-why-humans-matter

9   (i) Waxman, I. (2022). 'AI vs Lawyers - The Ultimate Showdown'. *Superlegal.* https://www.superlegal.ai/blog/aivslawyer/

(ii)Kita, J. (2024). 'Are You Ready for AI to Be a Better Doctor Than You?' *Medscape.* https://www.medscape.com/viewarticle/are-you-ready-ai-be-better-doctor-than-you-2024a100070q?form=fpf

10 Tubbs, W. (2024). 'Quantum computing and AI: The future of problem-solving'. *SAS Voices.* https://blogs.sas.com/content/sascom/2024/04/12/quantum-computing-and-ai/

11 (i) Lewis, B. (2023). 'Pisa: Wales Slumps to Worst School Test Results'. *BBC News*. 4 Dec. https://www.bbc.co.uk/news/uk-wales-67616536

(ii) Lancaster University (2020). 'Welsh-medium school pupils underperform in tests despite more advantaged backgrounds'. *phys.org*. https://phys.org/news/2020-09-welsh-medium-school-pupils-underperform-advantaged.html

12 (i) Classical Conversations (2022). 'What Is the Trivium? An Easy-to-Understand Analogy'. Classical Conversations. https://classicalconversations.com/blog/what-is-the-trivium/.

(ii) Lynch, P. (2017). 'Quadrivium: the noble fourfold way to an understanding of the universe'. The Irish Times. https://www.irishtimes.com/news/science/quadrivium-the-noble-fourfold-way-to-an-understanding-of-the-universe-1.3153793.

13 (i) Bayut (2021). 'Geometric Patterns in Islamic Art: Design and Meaning'. *MyBayut*. https://www.bayut.com/mybayut/islamic-art-geometric-patterns/

(ii) Hacker, S. (n.d.). 'Sacred Geometry in Christian Art'. *artway.eu*. https://artway.eu/artway.php?id=1169&action=show&lang=en

(iii) Watt, J. (2013). 'Himalayan Buddhist Art 101: Sacred Geometry, Part 1'. *Tricycle: The Buddhist Review*. https://tricycle.org/article/himalayan-buddhist-art-101-sacred-geometry-part-1/

(iv) Halai, C. (2019). 'Sacred Geometry Of Hindu Temples'. *Indica Today*. 22 Oct. https://www.indica.today/quick-reads/sacred-geometry-hindu-temples/

14 (i) BBC Learn & Revise (2023). 'The beauty of maths: Fibonacci and the Golden Ratio'. *BBC Bitesize*. https://www.bbc.co.uk/bitesize/articles/zm3rdnb

(ii) Rizzi, S. (2018). 'What is the Fibonacci Sequence – and why is it the secret to musical greatness?' *Classic FM*. https://www.classicfm.com/discover-music/fibonacci-sequence-in-music/

(iii) The Arch Insider (2020). 'Importance of Golden Ratio in Architecture'. *The Arch Insider*. https://thearchinsider.com/importance-of-golden-ratio-in-architecture/

(iv) Leary, C. (2019). 'How the Golden Ratio Manifests in Nature'. *Treehugger*. https://www.treehugger.com/how-golden-ratio-manifests-nature-4869736

(v) Meisner, G. (2012). 'Phi and the Solar System'. *Φ = Phi ≈ 1.618*. https://www.goldennumber.net/solar-system/

15 Blackburn, G. (2004). 'A Guide to Good Design'. *Fine Woodworking*. https://finewoodworking.com/FWNPDFfree/011168048.pdf

16 Bullitt County History Museum (n.d.). '1912 Eighth Grade Examination for Bullitt County Schools'. *Bullitt County History*. https://www.bullittcountyhistory.com/bchistory/schoolexam1912.html

17 Oltermann, P. (2019). 'Germany reintroduces "Meister" qualification for craftspeople'. *The Guardian*. https://www.theguardian.com/world/2019/dec/13/german-craftspeople-now-require-meister-qualification-to-start-business

18 American College of the Building Arts. (n.d.). 'About ACBA'. *American College of the Building Arts*. https://acba.edu/aboutacba

19 Forbes, P. (2010). 'The Case for Working with Your Hands by Matthew Crawford | Book review'. *The Guardian*. https://www.theguardian.com/books/2010/may/22/case-working-hands-michael-crawford

REBUILDING A
WELSH-SPEAKING WALES

As we work towards independence, we need a vision of what a free Wales will be like. An agreement on the fundamental aspects of our national identity and goals, which can be shared across the political spectrum, forming a foundation of shared values that can be above the cut and thrust of everyday politics.

One of these must be a commitment to making Wales a fully bilingual nation. The Welsh language is at the core of our history and identity. Without Y Gymraeg, who are we?

On that basis, how do we ensure the revival of Welsh as a community language? That means a language used in every aspect of life: in the home, in the workplace, in social settings. We will need to have policies that address every aspect of language use.

Let's start with the basics. Where will Welsh-speakers come from?

One source, of course, is children from Welsh-speaking families; individuals who have grown up speaking Welsh in the home. This group isn't sufficient for building numbers, though. Many will go through Welsh-medium education but then move into English-speaking social networks, work in English-speaking environments and marry someone who doesn't speak Welsh – and research shows that children who have only one Welsh-speaking parent generally don't go on to speak the language themselves. That's a serious cause of linguistic attrition.

The other source is non-speakers who acquire the language. The situation here is promising, as attitudes become more positive – helped by the efforts of the FAW to promote Welsh, new events such as Gŵyl Mabon, and others.

Future governments will need to implement policies which go far beyond the current 'Cymraeg 2050' framework.

The most obvious policy is to continue transitioning education to being bilingual and, ultimately, to being in Welsh. Like Toni Schiavone, I believe that this should become universal.[1] This policy alone will provide the basic linguistic foundation on which to build a Welsh-speaking country. However, the school system on its own isn't enough; too often, children at Welsh schools still speak English to each other,[2] and the problem of post-education attrition remains.

We also need to provide more help for adult learners – and to help adults become learners. I myself began speaking Welsh by attending a summer-long intensive Wlpan course. These are modelled on the intensive Hebrew courses that help migrants to Israel acquire the official language of their new nation.

This is the mindset that we in Wales must adopt; rather than seeing the Welsh Wlpan courses as something nice to do for those enthusiasts who can afford to attend, we need to see them as a fundamental element of building a truly bilingual nation – something to be encouraged; indeed, as something rather to be expected, and we shouldn't shy away from saying so. At some point, it may become a requirement for citizenship. To that end, we should legislate paid time off from work for learners to attend courses, much as we do with maternity leave.

However, an Wlpan course can only achieve so much. Immersion in the language needs to continue for learners to improve.

With this in mind, another model that Wales should adopt is that of the Moishe Houses, a movement that aims to strengthen the Jewish identity of young Jews, at a time in their lives when they are at risk of becoming a 'lost generation'.[3] Initially introduced in the US, Moishe Houses have now spread internationally, and the movement continue to grow.[4]

It's a simple idea: groups of early-career Jewish people share houses, as young people often do. Residents in Moishe Houses are given rent subsidies; in return, they commit to becoming an informal social hub, holding a given number of events every month, which they publicise and record on social media. The Moishe House Foundation raises the necessary funds from philanthropists and provides training and support to the residents to help them uphold their part of the deal.

The model is clearly applicable to building a Welsh-speaking nation. It would allow young people – whether new learners, people who attended a Welsh-medium school or those who grew up in Welsh-speaking homes – to keep on speaking Welsh at a critical period in their lives and develop strong Welsh-speaking social networks. Since this is also the age when people often meet their partner and settle down, it would significantly help to increase the number of families in which both parents speak Welsh. In the Welsh context, funding would have to come from government.

What about those who are older than this cohort and who want to improve their Welsh?

Here, I suggest that the Welsh Government's Welsh Language Service be given a much bigger national role and greater powers. At a micro level, it would standardise signage across the country, providing a uniform and correct Welsh wording for signs of all kinds, for example! At a macro level, it would establish a nation-wide, integrated tutoring program, intended to help learners and 'native speakers' alike engage in an ongoing process of improvement.

Organisations in independent Wales would be given support through subsidies and tax breaks to provide Welsh classes for staff as part of paid work time; businesses would be encouraged to make progress towards C2 (full proficiency) on the CEFR scale a contractual requirement. This would integrate the Welsh-at-work programs that already exist, and make them universal. (Of course, similar provision is needed to help people reach C2 in

English; research suggests that many Britons only have a B1 (intermediate) command of their native language – but that's for another time, perhaps.)

Business services such as 'Helo Blod' would be expanded and more heavily promoted.[5] There are already many such programs in place that address the use of Welsh in many ways. A bewildering number, in fact, few of which seem to be promoted very well. Let's integrate them and aggressively market a one-stop shop.

We could be even more radical. How about tax incentives for those who can demonstrate a C1/C2 command of Welsh? There could also be further tax breaks for families that speak Welsh in the home. Parents might receive similar incentives based on their children's linguistic ability.

Of course, there will be many complaints that all of this would be unfair for one reason or another. It wouldn't be.

The Cambridge English Dictionary defines 'fairness' as 'the quality of treating people equally or in a way that is right or reasonable'. We've perhaps become accustomed to thinking mostly in terms of the first element, equality. As a nation, though, we'll be thinking more in terms of the second: that policies which further our national goals are right and reasonable, and thus fair. After all, any kind of taxation and public spending could be seen as unfair in the first meaning, but we still choose to provide special needs education, social services and many other things – because that's the kind of society we choose to be.

So, let's be bold. Let's declare that we want Wales speaking Welsh, because that's who we are as a nation.

Many countries large and small do the same.[6] Let's set to work as a society and a country to make it happen, using all of the policy tools available to do so.

ENDNOTES

1   Schiavone, T. (2024). 'Universal Welsh medium education: It's possible'. *nation.cymru*. https://nation.cymru/opinion/universal-welsh-medium-education-its-possible/

2   Wightwick, A. (2023). 'Welsh school put in special measures as children found speaking too much English'. *WalesOnline*. https://www.walesonline.co.uk/news/education/welsh-school-put-special-measures-26147685

3   (i) (2024). 'Home'. *Moishe House*. https://www.moishehouse.org/

    (ii) Alperin, M. (2011). 'Moishe House Expanding to "Mecca for Young Adults", Bolstering its International Framework'. *eJewishPhilanthropy*. https://ejewishphilanthropy.com/moishe-house-expanding-to-mecca-for-young-adults-bolstering-its-international-framework/

4   (i) Merage Foundations (2014). 'Moishe House Strives to Meet International Expansion Demand for Young Jewish Adults – Establishes Global Community

Fund'. *www.prweb.com*. https://www.prweb.com/releases/2014/07/prweb12042438.htm

(ii) Rosenblatt, G. (2009). 'The 25 Houses Of Moishe, And Counting'. *Jewish Telegraphic Agency*. https://www.jta.org/2009/02/13/ny/the-25-houses-of-moishe-and-counting

5   Business Wales (n.d.). Helo Blod. https://businesswales.gov.wales/heloblod/helo-blod

6   (i) Ornstein, J. (1964). 'Patterns of Language Planning in the New States'. *World Politics*, 17(1). pp.40–49. https://doi.org/10.2307/2009386

(ii) Carter, B. and Sealey, A. (2007). 'Languages, Nations and Identities'. *Methodological Innovation Online*, 2(2). pp.20–31. https://doi.org/10.4256/mio.2007.0009

KEEPING CYMRU OUT OF NATO

Should an independent Cymru join NATO? In a recent article, Jeremy Brookman argued that it should.[1] I strongly disagree.

Several articles have already been published that attempt to identify the military resources Cymru should have on the basis of comparison to other small European nations.[2]

This, I think, is both premature and misguided. As Carl von Clausewitz famously observed, war is a tool used to achieve national goals once diplomatic methods have failed. We should plan on this basis.

For us in Wales, it's meaningless to discuss our future military without first agreeing what our national goals would actually be, what our diplomatic relations would be trying to achieve, and with whom.

An independent Cymru's force posture will have to address two questions:

1. What are our national security needs?

2. What funds and resources are available to establish and maintain an adequate response to those needs?

The first question needs to be broken down into three sub-topics:

I.   External security

II.   Internal security

III.   Economic security

These can't be separated from each other.

Given that we're talking about a newly independent country, money will be tight. We'll have to urgently spend large amounts on remedying London's long neglect of Welsh needs, notably making hundreds of unstable coal tips safe for the long term, but also addressing our appalling social deprivation. We'll probably need to redesign and relocate much of our national infrastructure, particularly the coastal railway lines that are close to the current sea level and are at risk. Things like this are essential and immediate priorities, but they will be very costly.

As a small country, we will need to maximise the number of people who are economically active, to help build a strong and sustainable economy. This must reflect the fact that our population is aging; we will have fewer and fewer military-age people, which will limit the numbers we can commit to our new armed forces.

In this context of straitened national resources, how do we address national security?

Both external and economic security will best be achieved by diplomatic means. Cymru will need to invest heavily in attracting the best and brightest to our new diplomatic service, able to negotiate the best trade deals and act as mediators and peacemakers.

What military threats will we face from outside? Even in a world that is becoming much more unstable, these are few. China has great ambitions, but its global force projection is aimed at keeping its trade routes secure, not conquest. Russia? Despite the fear-mongering in western capitals, Moscow poses no threat to Cymru.[3] Who, then? Realistically, there wouldn't be any pressing threats to our national territory.

A bigger issue will be border control with England. Will it be a hard border with fences, or a soft one? That will depend on political decisions. It may be that we will have free movement (if England also wants it: it wouldn't be our decision alone). However, if we choose to join the EEA, for example, but England doesn't, it would give us free movement and right of residence within the thirty member states. A hard border with England would be an acceptable price to pay for that.

Either way, cross-border crime will be a serious problem. Criminals involved in anything from the county lines drug gangs to thieves raiding Welsh farms would be able to escape back across the border to England and be beyond the reach of Welsh justice.[4]

What will we need in response? Large-scale drone surveillance. Communications intercepts and intelligence gathering. Rapid response and pursuit capacity, both airborne and ground-based. A coastguard that can not only rescue mariners in distress but can also pursue and apprehend whoever is throwing containers full of drugs into our seas.[5]

All of these internal security needs overlap with external security. It makes no sense to have two separate structures doing the same work. Post-independence, it would be better to reorganise on lines similar to those of France and other European nations. We would have a small national police force with a limited role, which would cover only the larger urban areas. Most current police functions would be transferred to a larger force of armed gendarmes, which would cover smaller communities and rural areas. The gendarmerie would have responsibility for border security, public order, roles such as anti-smuggling and counter-terrorism – and could act as infantry when needed for defence against external enemies.[6]

As noted, there aren't likely to be too many such enemies. So, should Cymru join NATO? No.

NATO was formed for mutual defence against the Soviet Union and its Eastern European allies. Both the USSR and the Warsaw Pact ceased to exist decades ago, and NATO should have gone with them. It's now an anachronism, serving no useful purpose.

This has been laid out in two reports published by the UK's Royal United Services Institute, established by the Duke of Wellington in 1831. The first report concludes that NATO member states no longer possess the industrial capability to wage war.[7] They cannot manufacture the munitions or equipment need for modern combat, and it would take decades of investment to rebuild that capacity. The second report starkly concludes that NATO's entire concept of war-fighting is outdated and unsuited to modern peer conflict.[8]

Not only do NATO countries lack adequate equipment and manpower; not only are their structures and tactics unfit for purpose (according to the Ukrainian soldiers who have received NATO training) but its entire concept of how to fight a war is obsolete.[9].

In short, NATO doesn't have the means to fight,[10] and wouldn't know how to if it did. Joining NATO would not protect Cymru and its people.

The picture that emerges from this thought experiment is of a small National Defence Force integrating land, sea and air operations, supplemented by a gendarmerie.

Since Azerbaijan defeated Armenia in 2020 with its use of drones, it's been clear that the future of warfare lies in drone swarms, missiles, air defence and electronic warfare, not tank regiments. This has been made even clearer by the progress of the conflict in Ukraine, and by the inability of NATO's high-tech warships and aircraft to counter the Yemeni Houthis' use of these low-cost methods in the Red Sea.

We will need coastguard cutters and some air capacity as well, of course. We will be well able to invest in the tools needed to defend our own land. We won't have the resources to fight elsewhere.

That, in turn, returns us to the conclusion that we will be better served by investing heavily in developing the best diplomatic service that we can and building strong relationships with those countries that supply the resources and markets we need to develop our economy. Most of them won't be in NATO, or even in the West; they'll be in Asia, Africa and the rest of the Global South.

As Palmerston observed, nations have no permanent friends or enemies, only permanent interests. NATO is a dinosaur, a relic from a different time and a different world. Joining it wouldn't advance our interests. Better to be neutral, to be able to defend our own land, and to build friendly links with all nations to promote the interests of Wales and its people.

ENDNOTES

1   Brookman, J. (2024). 'Plaid Cymru should commit an independent Wales to joining NATO'. *Bylines Cymru*. https://bylines.cymru/voices-lleisiau/nato-wales/

2   (i) Bowen, B. E. (2017). 'National security in an independent Wales: Intelligence and military considerations'. *nation.cymru*. https://nation.cymru/opinion/national-security-in-an-independent-wales-intelligence-and-military-considerations/

    (ii) Donovan, O. (2016). 'Defending Wales I: What does Wales need defending from?' *State of Wales*. https://stateofwales.com/2016/08/defending-wales-i-what-does-wales-need-defending-from/

3   Channon, M. (2022). 'Putin should "nuke" England but spare Wales, says Russian TV host'. *WalesOnline*. https://www.bbc.co.uk/news/uk-wales-46851815

4   (i) Thomas, R. and Jackson, C. (2018). 'County Lines: Why drug phenomenon has hit Wales so hard'. *BBC News*. 16 May. https://www.bbc.co.uk/news/uk-wales-44127068

(ii) BBC News (2020). 'Rural crime: Tractors and livestock taken as cost up in Wales'. *BBC News*. 4 Aug. https://www.bbc.co.uk/news/uk-wales-53641008

5   Hill, J. (2022). 'Suspected cocaine packages found washed up at multiple sites in Wales'. *Wales Online*. https://www.bbc.co.uk/news/uk-wales-46851815

6   (i) Anon. (2023). 'Law enforcement in France'. *Wikipedia*. https://en.wikipedia.org/wiki/Law enforcement in France

(ii) NATO Stability Policing (n.d.). 'French Gendarmerie'. NATO Stability Policing Centre of Excellence. https://www.nspcoe.org/about-us/sponsoring-nations/french-republic/french-gendarmerie/

7   Vershinin, A. (2022). 'The Return of Industrial Warfare'. rusi.org.   https://www.rusi.org/explore-our-research/publications/commentary/return-industrial-warfare

8   Vershinin, A. (2024). 'The Attritional Art of War: Lessons from the Russian War on Ukraine'. rusi.org. https://rusi.org/explore-our-research/publications/commentary/attritional-art-war-lessons-russian-war-ukraine

9   Follorou, J. (2023). 'Ukrainian soldiers trained abroad express discontent: "I repeatedly told them NATO manuals didn't apply"'. *Le Monde.fr*. 27 Sep. https://www.bbc.co.uk/news/uk-wales-46851815

10   Landale, J. (2023). 'Ukraine war: Western allies say they are running out of ammunition'. *BBC News*. 3 Oct. https://www.bbc.co.uk/news/world-europe-66984944

SILK ROADS, SALT ROUTES: CYMRU IN A BANDUNG WORLD

Let's picture the late 1390s and early 1400s, the years when Owain Glyndŵr was transformed from loyal subject of the English crown to rebel Prince of Wales.

People travelled. In Glyndŵr's time, knights, yeomen and peasants joined crusades against the Baltic pagans or the Turks threatening Hungary's borders. Others may have been to the Muslim Emirate of Granada and some to Constantinople, capital of the Eastern Roman Empire.

Although the mighty Mongol Empire was now fracturing into warring khanates, the Pax Mongolica of previous centuries had enabled trade from one end of Eurasia to the other via the Silk Routes.

The anonymous poet who wrote *Sir Gawain and the Green Knight* in Glyndŵr's lifetime referred to English castles decorated with tapestries from Turkmenistan – an area ruled by Emperor Timur, whose armies were then subduing northern India. A few years later, they would sweep west, crushing Ottoman armies and European crusaders alike, and conquering Persia on the way.

Further east, the Ming emperors were asserting Chinese power. As Glyndŵr's rebellion raged, a Muslim eunuch admiral, Zheng He, was beginning a series of expeditions. He would lead a vast fleet of Chinese ships – huge ships, which dwarfed anything known in Europe – through south-east Asia, to southern India and Sri Lanka, and onwards to Yemen and the Horn of Africa, enforcing imperial authority, collecting tribute and engaging in trade.

Visiting the Somali coast, Zheng would have met traders familiar with the routes that carried gold and salt across Africa, through the Orthodox Christian empire of Ethiopia, and across the Sahara and Sahel to the vastly wealthy Islamic empire of Mali. Both these empires had relations with the powerful Mamluk Emirs in Egypt. Iolo Goch wrote of Glyndŵr wearing 'feathers of the bird of Egypt' on his helmet while fighting in Scotland; these would have come from the peacocks which roamed his estate at Sycharth.

The world then was far more connected than we often realise – and the centre of wealth and power was Asia. Europe was in decline. By Glyndŵr's time, the crusader kingdoms in the Holy Land had long fallen; the thousand-year reign of Constantinople's Christian emperors would soon be ended by the Ottoman Turks.

We today may succeed where Glyndŵr failed; we may see Cymru become an independent sovereign state. If we do, we will join an international system with parallels to that of his time.

The power and influence of the West is fading; even friendly states, such as Singapore, say that this will be Asia's century.[1] Africa is shaking off the post-colonial economic structures that have kept it poor. With critical investments from Russia and China in ports, roads and railways, nuclear energy and hydropower, the continent could be on the brink of a massive renaissance, returning to the affluence – and influence – that its natural and human wealth justify.[2]

In 1955, countries from across Africa and Asia gathered in Bandung, Indonesia, to discuss how they could develop without getting caught up in the Cold War; it was the meeting that led to the Non-Aligned Movement. Today, that spirit is evident in the BRICS, including post-Soviet Russia and Iran. They're building a global economic system with its own financial and trade institutions, a system completely separate from the Western-dominated WTO, IMF and World Bank. They're building high-speed rail and sea-based transport routes stretching from Singapore to Beijing, Saint Petersburg to Mumbai, Vladivostok to Budapest.

I've heard people say that these countries depend on Western markets for their prosperity. I'm afraid this is a dangerously outdated view.

Brussels was sure that Russia's energy industry depended on EU sales, so the price cap and sanctions would collapse Russia's economy. They didn't. Washington thought its control of financial institutions meant it could 'turn the rouble into rubble'. Turns out it couldn't.

The EU is now making a similar mistake with China, threatening sanctions because of 'dumping' that undercuts European manufacturers. This misunderstands the reality that Chinese factories now operate on such a scale, and so efficiently, that the low prices are the natural outcome.

Western sanctions are backfiring. They are just stimulating local production – in Russia, aerospace; in China, microchips[3] – to become more advanced and cheaper than the West's products. The West is undercutting its own technological lead and will struggle to win it back, whilst still depending on Russian materials and parts.[4] While the West fusses about electric cars, China dominates that market – and launches electric ships.[5]

Wales will need to find a place in a global system dominated by Asia and Africa, not by the transatlantic countries. We'll need to find friends. Who might they be?

Wales has long-standing connections with Yemen as well as with Somaliland. In southern Africa, we have a strong connection with Lesotho.[6]

We have links with Russia:[7] Merthyr's John James Hughes founded the industrial city of Donetsk; Meirionnydd's General Henry Lloyd commanded armies for Catherine the Great, his innovative writings on strategy are still studied in Russian military academies.

In India, Wales has left the legacy of generations of missionaries.[8] A more secular connection is the contribution of philologist William Jones to standardising Sanskrit law, something that was recognised by Jawaharlal Nehru, independent India's first prime minister.[9]

In the Americas, our connection with Argentina, through the Welsh colony in Patagonia, needs no explanation. Our historical links with US states such as Pennsylvania, Tennessee and Idaho should be developed.

In Europe, we have an underappreciated ally in Hungary, where all schoolchildren learn a poem about Wales, *A Walesi Bardok* ('*The Bards of Wales*') by Janos Arany.[10] We have our Celtic cousins in Ireland, Scotland and Brittany. We have the goodwill and connections that come from the Six Nations Championship and other sporting tournaments.

Not all of these links are strong, but they are authentic and positive: foundations on which more concrete relationships can be built. Some of these countries – Yemen, Russia, Hungary – aren't popular today, but we'll do well to remember that though current governments and leaders will pass, the countries and their national interests will remain.

A Kenyan diplomat supposedly once said that 'every time China visits, we get a hospital; every time Britain visits, we get a lecture'. That may be apocryphal, but the sentiment is certainly true. Félix Tshisekedi, president of the Democratic Republic of Congo, openly says the same about the West,[11] as do other African leaders. Wales can't afford to behave like this.

As the ancient Chinese thinker Sūnzǐ (孙子) observed: without self-knowledge there's no success. We'll need to follow Singapore's example and have no illusions about being a small nation; 'As a small state, Singapore has no illusions about the state of our region or the world.'[12] We will have neither the right nor the means to tell other countries how to run their affairs. We'll need to accept that our political and cultural norms are not universal.

Nobody claims that independence will be easy. There will be hard choices to make. Like Glyndŵr, we must build relationships where we can. Our policies should be based on our nation's interests, not ideology.

Cymru, it's time to get real.

ENDNOTES

1   Suralta, B. B. (2023). 'Ex-U.N. Security Council President Kishore Mahbubani: "The 21st Century Belongs to Asia"'. *Esquire*. https://www.esquiremag.ph/politics/news/ex-united-nations-security-council-president-kishore-mahbubani-21st-century-asia-a00007-20230511-lfrm

2   (i) Nantulya, P. (2019). 'Implications for Africa from China's One Belt One Road Strategy'. *Africa Center for Strategic Studies*. https://africacenter.org/spotlight/implications-for-africa-china-one-belt-one-road-strategy/

       (ii) Neethling, T. (2019). 'How Russia is growing its strategic influence in Africa'. *The Conversation*. https://theconversation.com/how-russia-is-growing-its-strategic-influence-in-africa-110930

3   (i) Kaminski-Morrow, D. (2023). 'Russian regulator approves domestic wing and engines for MC-21'. *Flight Global*. https://www.flightglobal.com/aerospace/russian-regulator-approves-domestic-wing-and-engines-for-mc-21/151531.article

(ii) Udin, E. (2024). 'Qualcomm confirms that Huawei no longer need its chips'. *Gizchina.com*. https://www.gizchina.com/2024/05/11/huawei-no-longer-needs-qualcomm-chips/

4   (i) Reuters (2024). 'Airbus wins reprieve from Canadian sanctions on Russian titanium'. *Yahoo Finance*. https://finance.yahoo.com/news/airbus-wins-reprieve-canadian-sanctions-193102690.html

(ii) Terlep, S. (2024). 'Boeing's Latest Trouble Is a Jet Part Caught Up in Russia Sanctions'. *MSN*. https://www.msn.com/en-us/money/companies/boeing-s-latest-trouble-is-a-jet-part-caught-up-in-russia-sanctions/ar-AA1o59E8

5   (i) Williams, K. (2024). 'I Went To China And Drove A Dozen Electric Cars. Western Automakers Are Cooked'. *InsideEVs*. https://insideevs.com/features/719015/china-is-ahead-of-west/

(ii) Lopez, J. (2024). 'China Launches World's Largest Electric Container Ship, Slashing 8,600 Pounds of Emissions per 100 Nautical Miles'. *Tech Times*. https://www.techtimes.com/articles/304092/20240429/china-launches-worlds-largest-electric-container-ship.htm

6   (i) Hancock, G. (2024). 'The Yemenis of Cardiff: Britain's oldest Muslim diaspora'. *Middle East Eye*. https://www.middleeasteye.net/discover/yemen-cardiff-uk-oldest-muslim-diaspora

(ii) Mansfield, M. (2023). 'Celebrating Somaliland's Independence Day in Wales – a triumph for diversity'. *Nation.Cymru*. https://nation.cymru/opinion/celebrating-somalilands-independence-day-in-wales-a-triumph-for-diversity/

(iii) Williams, P. (2008). 'Wales' African Twin The story of Dolen Cymru - the Wales Lesotho Link'. *Dolen Cymru*. https://www.dolencymru.org/wp-content/uploads/2021/05/walesafricantwindolencymru.pdf

7   (i) Lowe, A. (2009). 'Welsh Adventurer Henry Lloyd'. *Warfare History Network*. https://warfarehistorynetwork.com/article/welsh-adventurer-henry-lloyd/

(i) Duffy, S. (2017). 'Hughesovka: The city founded by Welsh migrants'. *BBC News*. 30 Jun. https://www.bbc.co.uk/news/uk-wales-40345030

8   Owens, D. (2024). 'Exploring the history of the Welsh relationship with India'. *Nation.Cymru*. https://nation.cymru/culture/exploring-the-history-of-the-welsh-relationship-with-india/

9   Ehrlich, J. and Stewart, I. (2023). 'New Perspectives on the Life and Worlds of Sir William Jones', *Global Intellectual History*, pp.1–7. doi:10.1080/2380188 3.2023.2184409

10 BBC News (2017). 'Hungary celebrates legendary tale of Welsh bards' slaughter'. *BBC News*. 2 Mar. https://www.bbc.co.uk/news/uk-wales-mid-wales-39136034

11   Fulani, R. (2024). 'Félix Tshisekedi sur LCI: « La Russie et la Chine en Afrique se comportent mieux que les Occidentaux »'. *NOUVEAUMEDIA.CD*. https://www.nouveaumedia.cd/felix-tshisekedi-sur-lci-la-russie-et-la-chine-en-afrique-se-comportent-mieux-que-les-occidentaux/

12   Ministry of Foreign Affairs (n.d.). 'Foreign Policy'. *Ministry of Foreign Affairs*. www.mfa.gov.sg. https://www.mfa.gov.sg/Overseas-Mission/Bangkok/About-Singapore/Foreign-Policy

DRUIDS ON THE SILK ROAD

In 1921, both of my paternal grandparents turned twenty-one and became legal adults. In that year, the Welsh coal industry was booming from pent-up post-war demand. Its customers were all over the world, and that meant ships were needed to transport it; new shipping companies were being set up throughout South Wales, often several each week. Most owned only one or two vessels, and much of their capital came from ordinary Welsh people, from miners to chapel congregations. Their crews were often 100% Welsh-speaking. Wales was prosperous.

The Great War had formally ended in 1918, but much of the world continued to experience the fallout.

The British Army had only just left Crimea, where it had been supporting counter-revolutionary forces under Baron Pyotr Wrangel, the last White Russian commander in the west. Admitting defeat, Wrangel gathered the remnants of the Imperial Black Sea Fleet and evacuated nearly 150,000 soldiers and civilians to Constantinople, where they faced a bleak future as stateless refugees.

Constantinople was still the seat of the Ottoman sultan. Most of his empire had been lost; the Turkish heartland was being fought over by Greeks supported by other Western powers on the one hand and the Ottoman general who had defeated the British at Gallipoli, Mustafa Kemal Pasha, on the other.

Further east, in modern Uzbekistan, another former Ottoman leader was commanding a cavalry army of tribal nomads trying to establish Turkestan: a new commonwealth of Turkic Muslim peoples stretching from the Caspian Sea, through Central Asia, to what is now the western part of Xinjiang in China. He was Enver Pasha.

Further east again, the last Tsarist commander still in the field was Baron Roman Ungern von Sternberg. Unable to hold out against the Red Army, he had led his Asiatic Cavalry Division from Siberia into Mongolia. His men were a motley assembly of White Russian cavalry, Cossacks, and Buryat nomads, supplemented by Japanese adventurers. Having joined forces with the Mongols, along with Tibetan cavalry sent by the Dalai Lama, they had driven out the forces of Republican China, restoring Mongolian independence under the theocratic rule of the blind Buddhist monk and poisoner, the Bogd Khan. Sternberg dreamed of establishing a new Buddhist nomad empire, stretching from Manchuria in the east, westwards through Mongolia and southern Siberia, then into eastern Xinjiang and Tibet.

Both Wrangel and Sternberg were ethnic Germans, born into the aristocracy that had ruled the Baltic nations since the Middle Ages. Their ancestors were Teutonic Knights, crusaders against the pagan tribes there, who settled to create the Duchy of Livonia. After the Tsars annexed the region, the *Deutschbalten* served them faithfully for centuries, often rising to the highest ranks.

Sternberg's wife was a member of the ethnic Manchu aristocracy that had ruled China under the Qing dynasty for two and a half centuries until the Republican revolution of 1911. The deposed Manchu emperor, Puyi, was now fifteen years old and still lived in the Forbidden City. His advisors debated whether or not he should flee to his ancestral homeland in Manchuria and declare a new empire formed from Manchuria, Mongolia and Tibet – regions that weren't part of historical China but which owed their allegiance personally to the Qing emperors. The Bogd Khan, Sternberg and his army, and thousands of other White Russian exiles would support him, as would Japan.

All of this is historical fact. What does it teach us? That dramatic changes can occur suddenly and unexpectedly – and we forget that too easily. Ten years earlier, in 1911, none of the people I've described could have any idea how their world would be turned upside down. Very few reading this will have had any idea that the world of 1921 was so very unlike 2021, or that if a few key events had unfolded in other ways, our world today would be unimaginably different.

It's also that national and personal identities are in some ways very fluid, and in some ways very, very enduring.

With Anglo-Welsh culture now on its deathbed,[1] any independent Cymru will unavoidably be different from today's Wales. That Cymru will, of necessity, be powered by a revival of cultural confidence and vitality amongst Welsh-speakers and learners.

What kind of world will that Cymru exist in?

Those hoping to join the EU are likely to be disappointed, as the centrifugal tensions within the Union are already putting it under strain. Older sympathies and identities are re-emerging. Poland and the Baltic states have a long history via the Polish-Lithuanian Commonwealth; Hungary and Slovakia are already becoming closer to non-EU Serbia, and Austria could well collaborate with them in forming a 'Habsburg Group' – all have been uncomfortable with the EU's policies regarding the conflict in Ukraine, as well as with Brussels' centralising efforts and its imposition of transatlantic cultural values. All, in various ways, are edging closer to the Sino-Russian BRICS group.

Key to Europe's future will be Germany. It may form part of the core for a reduced EU – a new 'Charlemagne' zone with France and Italy. Indeed, given the enduring disparities between the former East and West,[2] it's not inconceivable that Germany might once again split. Bismarck's unified German state is, after all, another relatively recent creation, and its continued existence isn't written in stone. Serbia, Romania, Bulgaria and Greece may find their shared Orthodox Christianity drawing them closer to a newly powerful 'Holy Russia'.[3]

Outside Europe, the non-Western world is integrating in a way that hasn't been seen for centuries.

In the time of Owain Glyndŵr, China sent enormous trading fleets through south-east Asia and on to India and East Africa.[4] Today, the Belt and Road Initiative (BRI) is improving connectivity across Eurasia, connecting

Serbia, Hungary and Germany with the manufacturers and markets of China. Meanwhile, it will soon be possible to travel from Beijing to Singapore entirely by high-speed train.[5] The BRI is also building up trading links between east Asia, the Indian subcontinent, the Middle East and East Africa, reviving the connections made by those ancient fleets. From the ports on the Horn of Africa, Chinese investment revives the ancient gold and salt route across the Sahel to the Atlantic.[6] Russia is also actively developing the International North-South Transport Corridor, connecting its ports in the Baltic with Iran and India.[7]

This will be a Bandung world: a world that emphasises sovereignty, non-intervention, equality between countries and peaceful economic development.[8] This world will be dominated by the resource-rich nations of Asia and Africa, deriving security from the military power of the Sino-Russian alliance and with economic growth driven by the industrial power of China. The countries of the global West – NATO and its allies – will increasingly be excluded and will have to work with their own dwindling resources.

What of independent Cymru in this global context?

In this collection of essays, I've engaged in scenario planning based on current trends. Certain themes keep showing up, and a picture of future Cymru begins to emerge.

One recurring theme is that we will need to establish a substantial Welsh merchant fleet. We'll need to invest in reviving the ports all round our coast, making them commercially active again. This will re-enable logistics chains delivering communities' needs as resource shortages make the road network unmaintainable. It will also establish our international water trade, transporting clean water to where it's needed by means of Dracone barges.

Transporting that water to the ports will require infrastructure; this work will go alongside investment to relocate our railways, moving them away from the low-lying areas which are threatened by sea level rise. This threat will also require substantial investment in sea walls and, potentially, the relocation of entire communities to higher land. This may be regarded as an opportunity to revitalise the decaying towns and villages of the Valleys; it may be that entirely new settlements will need to be established.

This, however, could be a problem, given the anticipated shortages of concrete and other sand-based materials. It may not be possible to build the new roads or upgrade existing roads to current standards. Potentially, it may not even be possible to build new housing on current models. Cymru will therefore need to invest very heavily in developing new building materials that can be sustainably produced for the long term.

Another investment that will be urgently needed is the construction of tidal power lagoons in both the north and south of the country. This clean, sustainable and – most importantly – dependable energy will make our own economy energy-independent, and may well provide substantial export revenues.

We should do our utmost to attract the manufacturers of both amphibious aircraft and airships to establish themselves here. Far-sighted and early investment here will not only create skilled jobs, it will provide us with the means to sustain our communities as land-based infrastructure crumbles, as well as generating export opportunities.

Trends in geopolitics, resource depletion and energy availability all indicate that our economy will become much more localised. The products we use will increasingly be made from materials that are produced or recycled here, and will be sold by local retailers rather than big-box superstores – whose business model will no longer work.

This will transform our agricultural sector – and hence our landscape – beyond recognition.

With diesel, artificial fertiliser and imported corn rising dramatically in price, intensive farming will come to an end, to be replaced by regenerative farming techniques. This will be supplemented with rewilding where possible, which will not only revive biodiversity but will create new and diversified revenue streams for farmers. An important part of this will be the regeneration of the Celtic rainforest.

More significantly, farming practices will have to change, possibly dramatically. As the climate changes, so too will our weather. More rainfall seems inevitable. Temperatures may rise, but if the Gulf Stream shuts down – which is possible according to scientific models – Cymru may actually become colder than it is today, even while much of the world gets hotter. Either way, we will probably find ourselves adopting new forms of farming, such as growing rice rather than wheat and raising water buffaloes as well as cows.

Agriculture will become more labour-intensive; we'll need to look at ways of turning 'agricultural worker' into a meaningful career. Welsh-medium schools will become more closely integrated into the farming community once more – not only learning countryside skills, but studying the changes brought about by rewilding, developing craft skills, learning about the links between their community and the natural environment in which it exists.

That education will also have shifted away from the current model, which is out of date, and will be constructed around the seven liberal arts. Going to university will be less common compared to receiving a craft or trade education; those who do go will go later, after coming to understand what they really want to do.

This bilingual education system, combined with the liberal arts, will be designed to emphasise cultural intelligence and cross-cultural mediation skills. This is something we will develop as a national speciality, holding mediation 'festivals' to complement the international cultural prominence of the Llangollen Eisteddfod.

Bilingualism will, of course, be a core national priority for independent Cymru. Transitioning to being a country that once again uses the Welsh language in all spheres will be supported through the use of all available policy tools. These will include delivering all compulsory education through the medium of Welsh, providing paid time off to learn Welsh on the same model as maternity leave and expanding access to Wlpan courses. Financial support will be given to early-career workers to form Welsh-speaking house-shares, and tax incentives will be given both to individuals who demonstrate full command of the language and to households with children where Welsh is the language of the home.

Given financial, demographic and other constraints on our resources, national security will be centred on a small, unified Welsh Defence Force rather than having separate services. To maximise efficiency, Cymru will move to a European internal security and policing model, with a gendarmerie taking over most policing and border responsibilities, and the current civilian police force focusing on the metropolitan areas only.

Cymru will also need to find its place in the world. As I write, it's clear that the post-WW2 international order is coming to an end. The economic and military predominance of the United States and its allies is fading away, to be replaced by a multipolar system in which Russia, China, Iran and India are also major players. This will very probably be accompanied by an economic renaissance across Asia, Africa and Latin America as governments across the Global South reclaim control of their natural assets and use their wealth for their own development. Both NATO and the EU, meanwhile, stand a good chance of fracturing into smaller blocs; some of these will align themselves with the United States, while others will become more integrated with the BRICS and China's Belt and Road Initiative.

So, where should Cymru seek to establish itself in the international community?

I cannot see that we will receive any goodwill from London. We know that much of England's establishment despises Wales and its culture; Westminster has systematically robbed us of our wealth whilst underfunding our needs. We know that they would regard Welsh independence as a humiliation. In no realistic scenario could an independent Cymru regard a resentful England as a reliable partner. What about the rest of the Western world? Let's put it this way: after leaving the EU, Westminster has failed to obtain trade deals with either the United States or Canada. The deal it reached with Australia benefitted Australian exporters far more than their British counterparts. If the UK cannot obtain good deals from its Anglophone 'allies', what chance would Cymru have? And why would we want to align our nation with the neo-liberal system that the Anglosphere represents, but which has brought such desperate poverty and deprivation to Welsh communities?

Wales has been treated by London as a colony, something we share with all of the former colonies that now compose the Global South. The economy of independent Cymru will largely be based on resources – our water and energy in particular, though we will have some manufacturing. By the time we achieve independence, it's likely that Westminster's policies will have collapsed the Welsh university sector and associated industries; we will have many highly educated and highly skilled people in economic distress. They will likely join our doctors, dentists, nurses and other essential workers in emigrating, causing a brain drain and presenting us with a major economic and social crisis. In all of these things, we have much in common with those same former colonies. Like them, we will need to practise resource nationalism – if companies want to benefit from our water or electricity, we will require them to set up in Cymru, employing Welsh workers.

All of this indicates that Cymru will be best served by joining the BRICS group and the Belt and Road Initiative. This is going to be resisted by those whose minds have been colonised the most, who believe that we culturally have more in common with England and the other countries of the Anglosphere. As we foster the regrowth of the Welsh language, though, and as we implement policies that detach us from neo-liberalism in favour of our own people's interests, that really isn't going to be the case anymore, and that isn't going to make England or the US love us; it will make us more alien, and they will resent it.

Cymru will once again become a confident, Welsh-speaking nation, proud of a history that stretches back to the Atlantic mariners of the Bronze Age and a culture that has survived challenge after challenge for centuries. We will reach beyond Europe to seek opportunities and friends on the ancient Silk Roads of Asia and on the Salt Routes of Africa. We knew this world when the Druids travelled to Afghanistan; we knew it when Glyndŵr dealt with – and possibly died with – the Knights Hospitallers of the Middle East. We knew it when John James Hughes and Henry Lloyd went to Russia; we knew it when William Jones went to Bengal. Independence will bring challenges, but we've faced worse. It was worse when Magnus Maximus stripped Britain of her legions, and worse when Flavius Aetius refused to bring them back. It was worse when Llywelyn fell at Cilmeri, and worse when Glyndŵr's rebellion failed. We survived all of those. We will survive and thrive as an independent nation.

We will do more than thrive. We will realise Saunders Lewis's vision of a true Welsh civilisation, with our own values and institutions. We won't try to force anyone to be like us, and we will resist – as we have always resisted – those who try to force us to be like them. We will form a piece of the mosaic of nations; each piece unique and individual, but together forming a harmonious whole.

And Welsh Druids will once again travel the Silk Road.

ENDNOTES

1   Phillips, E. (2024). 'Losing a Welsh identity: Reform UK and a changing Wales'. *Bylines Cymru*. https://bylines.cymru/voices-lleisiau/reform-uk-in-wales/

2   Connolly, K. (2020). '"Germany looks like it's still divided": stark gaps persist 30 years after reunification'. *The Guardian*. 16 Sep. https://www.theguardian.com/world/2020/sep/16/germany-east-west-gaps-persist-30-years-reunification

3   Cherniavsky, M. (1958). '"Holy Russia": A Study in the History of an Idea'. *The American Historical Review*, 63(3). pp.617–637. https://doi.org/10.2307/1848883

4   The Editors of Encyclopaedia Britannica. (2020). 'Zheng He's Achievements'. *Encyclopedia Britannica*. 23 Sep. https://www.britannica.com/summary/Zheng-Hes-Achievements

5   Chen, H. (2024). 'China is trying to connect Southeast Asia by high-speed rail. Here's how that's going'. *MSN*. www.msn.com. https://www.msn.com/en-us/news/world/china-is-trying-to-connect-southeast-asia-by-high-speed-rail-here-s-how-that-s-going/ar-BB1kwVAK

6   Department of the Arts of Africa, Oceania and the Americas (2000). 'The Trans-Saharan Gold Trade (7th–14th Century)'. *Metmuseum.org.* https://www. metmuseum.org/toah/hd/gold/hd_gold.htm

7   Cheema, G. (2020). 'The International North-South Transport Corridor: Shifting Gears in Eurasian Connectivity'. *Modern Diplomacy.* https:// moderndiplomacy.eu/2020/09/24/the-international-north-south-transport-corridor-shifting-gears-in-eurasian-connectivity/

8   Office of the Historian (2019). 'Bandung Conference (Asian-African Conference), 1955'. *US Department of State.* https://history.state.gov/milestones/1953-1960/bandung-conf

AUTHOR PROFILE

Emlyn Phillips is an author, coach and sense-maker, not to mention a trained hypnotherapist and mediator. In the course of a globe-trotting career, he has been one of the first bilingual web developers in Wales, a corporate coach in Singapore, an English teacher for corporate clients in Russia, and a university lecturer in both Beijing and Swansea. With a BA (Hons) in International Relations, an MSc in Computer Science, and an MBA and Postgraduate Certificate with Honours in Applied Linguistics, he is very much a cross-disciplinary thinker.

His website is https://traethiad.com

He can be found on X @emlyn_yunfei

***

What Did You Think of *Druids on the Silk Road*?

A big thank you for purchasing this book. It means a lot that you chose this book specifically from such a wide range on offer. I do hope you enjoyed it.

Book reviews are incredibly important for an author. All feedback helps them improve their writing for future projects and for developing this edition. If you are able to spare a few minutes to post a review on Amazon, that would be much appreciated.

Publisher Information

rowanvale books

Rowanvale Books provides publishing services to independent authors, writers and poets all over the globe. We deliver a personal, honest and efficient service that allows authors to see their work published, while remaining in control of the process and retaining their creativity. By making publishing services available to authors in a cost-effective and ethical way, we at Rowanvale Books hope to ensure that the local, national and international community benefits from a steady stream of good quality literature.

For more information about us, our authors or our publications, please get in touch.

www.rowanvalebooks.com
info@rowanvalebooks.com